ZAGARE

Litvaks and Lithuanians Confront the Past

SARA MANOBLA

gefen
publishing house בית הוצאה לאור
JERUSALEM ◆ NEW YORK
Est. 1981

Cover Design: Leah Ben Avraham/Noonim Graphics
Typesetting: Irit Nachum
Map prepared by Talya Shachar-Albocher

ISBN: 978-965-229-657-3

1 3 5 7 9 8 6 4 2

Quotations from Ellen Cassedy, *We Are Here: Memories of the Lithuanian Holocaust* (Lincoln: University of Nebraska Press, 2012); Dovid Katz, www. defendinghistory.com; Bernard Wasserstein, *Vanishing Diaspora: The Jews in Europe since 1945* (London: Penguin Books, 1997); and Rose Zwi, *Last Walk in Naryshkin Park* (North Melbourne, Victoria: Spinifex Press, 1997) and *Once Were Slaves: A Journey through the Circles of Hell* (Darlinghurst, New South Wales: Sydney Jewish Museum, 2010) reproduced by permission of the authors.

Gefen Publishing House Ltd.	Gefen Books
6 Hatzvi Street	11 Edison Place
Jerusalem 94386, Israel	Springfield, NJ 07081
972-2-538-0247	516-593-1234
orders@gefenpublishing.com	orders@gefenpublishing.com

www.gefenpublishing.com

Printed in Israel   *Send for our free catalog*

Library of Congress Cataloging-in-Publication Data

Manobla, Sara.
Zagare : Litvaks and Lithuanians confront the past / Sara Manobla.
   pages cm
Includes bibliographical references.
ISBN 978-965-229-657-3
1. Jews—Lithuania—Zagare—History. 2. Jews—Persecutions—Lithuania—
Zagare. 3. Holocaust, Jewish (1939-1945)—Lithuania—Zagare. 4. Holocaust,
Jewish (1939-1945)—Anniversaries, etc. 5. Lithuania—Ethnic relations.
6. Memory—Social aspects. 7. Memorials—Lithuania—Zagare. I. Title.
DS135.L5M36 2014
940.53'18094793—dc23
                                         2014001183

FOR JOY AND VALDAS

without whom none of this would have happened

CONTENTS

Could I honor my heritage without perpetuating
the fears and hatreds of those who came before?

Ellen Cassedy, *We Are Here: Memories of the Lithuanian Holocaust*

PREFACE

This is a story of facing and coming to terms with history. Accepting Zagare was something all of us found ourselves doing – in Zagare – on July 13, 2012. From its inception the project of erecting a plaque in the town square commemorating the annihilation in 1941 of the town's entire Jewish community was a joint undertaking by Jews of Zagarean descent together with local Lithuanians led by Valdas Balciunas. At no stage was it a gesture of revenge or a settling of accounts. Accepting, acknowledging, remembering and educating – these were our goals.

In a letter written after we returned home from Zagare, one of our group, filmmaker Rod Freedman, wrote: "I think the word *reconciliation* is appropriate – for me personally and because of Valdas's attitude and other non-Jews whom we met. We're not talking about meeting with the perpetrators; it's almost too late for that now, so it's not about reconciling with those who participated, or about forgiving. For me, it's about acknowledgement and showing respect."

Paying tribute to those noble Lithuanians who risked their lives and the lives of their families to save Jews in distress was also part of our mission. The testimony of Ruth Yoffe, a Holocaust survivor living in Jerusalem, would enable us to pay homage to a Zagarean family who had rescued her and her grandmother Batya: the Levinskas family were to be honored by the Yad Vashem Holocaust Martyrs' and Heroes' Remembrance Authority as

Righteous among the Nations and would be remembered on our memorial dedication day alongside those who had been killed.

We were a group of eight, descendants of families that had left Zagare – in good time – before World War II. Our ancestors had fled in order to escape persecution and make a better life for their children. We came from England, America, South Africa, Australia and Israel looking for roots and for a connection with a place and history inherited from our parents and grandparents. Each of us had a different perception of Zagare and what it meant to us. My initial engagement developed through my interest in Jewish genealogy and family history; it continued through my involvement with the struggle of Soviet Jewry, promoting the cause of refuseniks who wished to immigrate to Israel.

There were those in our little band who had come to say Kaddish for their relatives murdered in 1941 and to lay a flower on the mass grave. There were those who genuinely wished to reach out to the young generation of the town and help them to improve their lives. When we met in Zagare we all found ourselves striving to come to terms with the perceptions of other people we met on the way. *Acceptance* could be an all-embracing word for this process of coming to terms and for what I would like to believe we accomplished – not forgiving, not forgetting, but a measure of tolerance, respect, hope, listening, supporting, agreeing, accepting and letting go, all sorely needed in our world today.

Jerusalem, 2014

ACKNOWLEDGMENTS

First my most grateful thanks to those who have allowed me to quote from their writings, published and unpublished: Valdas Balciunas, Julius Bieliauskas, Aldona Bagdoniene, Ellen Cassedy, Rod Freedman, Alex Gibb, Joy Hall, Dovid Katz, Leonidas Levinskas, Cliff Marks, Sarah Mitrike, Suki Pay, Bernard Wasserstein, Len Yodaiken and Rose Zwi. All were important players in the events I have recounted, and all have given me invaluable support and encouragement in the writing of this book. My debt to Ruth Yoffe for her readiness to share her memories and photos with me is inestimable. Yad Vashem gave permission to quote from their archives.

Rod Freedman graciously allowed me to use three of his excellent photographs: Isaac Mendelssohn bemedaled, the plaque in the town square, and the mass grave. For the book cover, Aleksandrs Feigmanis gave me permission to include his photograph of Isaac by the Zagare road sign; the picture of me was taken by my granddaughter Rona Gabrielle Abadi, and the cherries came from Joy Hall. The picture of Joy, Suki and Isaac beside the memorial obelisk and the picture of me interviewing President Adamkus also came from Joy; the Zagare synagogue photo was taken by Zilvinas Beliauskas. The early photographs came from family albums, and the 1925 Zagare street scene postcard on the cover from the archive of Aron Segal. The rest of the pictures are mine.

Sheryl Abbey, Ellen Cassedy, Herbert Krosney, Sarah Mitrike and Neville Teller read the manuscript in various stages of progress, pointed out mistakes and gave me invaluable help with their advice and comments. Allan Blacher's website with the marvelous family tree enabled me to track down Ruth Yoffe and obtain the testimony required by Yad Vashem. My editors Kezia Raffel Pride, Ita Olesker, Lynn Douek and Evelyn Grossberg spotted many inaccuracies and infelicities in the text, and suggested a number of improvements. My thanks also go to the Remember and Save Association, http://www.soviet-jews-exodus.com, for allowing me to quote from Aba Taratuta's interview with Viktor Brailovsky; to Yad Vashem researcher Katya Gusarov; to Ambassador Hagit Ben Ya'akov; to Deputy Head of Mission Liat Wexelman; and to the staff at the Israeli embassy in Riga.

CHAPTER ONE

FAMILY

G rowing up in the north of England, surrounded by aunts and uncles, I knew nothing of my ancestry. I have a fleeting memory of Grandpa Towb, of sitting on his knee, my forehead tickled by his white beard, at a family gathering, perhaps Seder night, at the Wingrove Road family home in Newcastle. But I was too young to ask questions about life in *der heim*, the "old country." I knew that Grandpa was an immigrant – the heavy accent betrayed that – and my understanding was that he came from Russia. "Why didn't Grandpa teach you Russian?" I once asked my Dad. "Russian?" he said. "My father didn't speak Russian." I was puzzled. How could you live in a country and not speak the language? "So what did he speak?" "Yiddish, of course," said Dad, and that was the end of the conversation. Nobody mentioned Lithuania. The Baltic states had disappeared from the atlas, swallowed up in the Soviet Union, the great monolith that had taken over from the Tsarist Empire, where Grandpa and his brothers were born and from which they had fled.

Grandma Towb, Berthe or Batya Moeller, was born in Zagare, Lithuania, in 1865, and it was there, in 1889, that she married David

▲ Lithuania and surrounding regions (modern borders)

Towb. He was born in Baisogala, also in Lithuania, in 1863, the third of four brothers. They all bore different surnames, a common occurrence in Jewish families at that time, when compulsory military service meant years of separation from home. There was an exemption for one child, usually the eldest son, so the younger boys approaching conscription age would take on new names and identities, preparing to emigrate to the West.

The reactionary Tsar Alexander III began his reign in 1881 with a wave of pogroms, which ushered in a period of severe repression for the Jews of Russia and the Russian-controlled Baltic states. A massive emigration followed; South Africa and the United States were the favored destinations, with some émigrés heading for Europe or for Palestine. By 1891, in the wake of another series of violent pogroms, more than one million Jews had fled Russia and the adjacent Russian-controlled territories.

Grandpa left Zagare in February 1890, armed with a passport issued by the Russian military authorities in Siauliai. We don't know if this document would have indicated whether he had completed his military service, was liable for reserve duty, or was exempt. Perhaps he was a deserter, unwilling to fight in the reserves now that he was married. It is very probable that he crossed the border out of Russia illegally. A family legend has it that he traveled to Belgium by sled or on foot across the frozen waters of the Baltic Sea. Looking at the map I thought this was improbable so I posted a query on LitvakSIG, a discussion group offshoot of the JewishGen website, and asked for suggestions.

The replies opened up a rich insight into the journeys our ancestors had made in the 1890s, as they headed west from the Pale of Settlement towards a new life in a new country. In this period, following the pogroms, vast numbers of Jews were on the move, by boat, train, carriage or on foot. If Grandpa had indeed slithered in his boots across the ice towards freedom, the most likely route, according to one of the LitvakSIG suggestions, would have been crossing the Curonian Lagoon, a shallow body of water just inland from the Baltic Sea. The lagoon invariably freezes over in winter and in that period it formed the frontier with Prussia. He would have reached the German town of Memel, known also as Klaipeda, a major port city and commercial center situated at the northern end of the lagoon. From here he could have traveled by train to Hamburg and continued on to Antwerp where his two older brothers, Israel Friedlander and Myer Israelovich, were already living with their families.

Israel and Myer had established a hostelry in Antwerp, the Hotel Friedlander, patronized largely by Jewish émigrés heading west. Grandpa left behind in Zagare his wife and their newborn son Ya'akov, my uncle Jack. Some six months later Grandpa took the boat from Antwerp to Hull, and from there made his way to Swansea. Why he left his brothers, why he settled in Great Britain and not America or South Africa is not known. There are stories of boats docking at port towns on the east coast of England or Scotland, where gullible travelers disembarked, believing they had arrived in New York.

Grandpa Towb appears in the 1891 census for Wales, listed as David Taub, age twenty-eight, birthplace Russia, a picture frame dealer and a lodger at 158 Llangyfelach Street, Swansea. From this point on our family history unfolds in Britain. Grandma and Uncle Jack made the journey from Zagare – presumably with legal passports – to join Grandpa in Wales. In Swansea six more children were born: Harry in 1892, followed by Rebecca, Leah, my father William, Massie and Louis. Tragically, soon after the birth of the youngest, Grandma died, and Grandpa was left to cope with a brood of seven young children. Following a brief return to Antwerp, Grandpa moved his family to Gateshead in the northeast of England and some years later settled in Newcastle upon Tyne. Here my father met Sylvia Jacobs, they fell in love and were married. In 1934 I was born and named Ursula Sara Towb, joined in 1936 by my sister Elisabeth.

Zagare was forgotten, never mentioned. In the north of England Grandpa, my father, my uncle Louis, and two of Grandpa's sons-in-law made a living in the scrap metal business. This entailed buying scrap metal from itinerant pushcart collectors and reselling the metal to the foundries and shipyards of the Tyneside shipbuilding industry. There were no partnerships in the family; each breadwinner was on his own and had his own premises – a yard for dumping and sorting, a shed for storing the scrap metal, and an office with a desk and a chair for negotiating transactions. It was hard, dirty work, and at first they struggled to make a living. But they all managed, somehow, to establish themselves and provide for their families. Then came World War II, and with shipbuilding on Tyneside and increased production of armaments it was a good period for scrap metal merchants.

With growing prosperity Grandpa and his children had moved from Gateshead to Newcastle across the River Tyne, a step up the ladder towards the middle class. By now Grandpa, needing someone to help with raising the family, had remarried. It was an arranged match, and Grandpa saw his bride – Aunt Rose, as we called her – for the first time under the *chuppah*, the marriage canopy. The new union was not a great success. Aunt Rose was neither beautiful nor clever, and not much of a homemaker. Her stepchildren made fun of her, and we called her "Poor Aunt Rose." Grandpa told my uncle Louis that the marriage was never consummated. But it endured; divorce was a rare occurrence in those days. After Grandpa's death the stepchildren looked after Aunt Rose and we continued to visit her. I still have an embroidered pink satin pajama case that she gave me as a birthday present.

One by one the Towb offspring married and left home. As a

child I didn't know my uncle Jack, who lived in Ireland, nor my uncle Harry, who had settled in South Africa. But the remaining members of the family were a close-knit bunch, and we of the generation of Grandpa's grandchildren numbered thirteen first cousins. The aim of our parents was for us to succeed in this new world where Grandpa had put down his roots – and to become British. Success meant money in the bank together with education, and the two went hand in hand. I was the first member of the family to graduate from university, a source of much pride to everyone.

Ours was not an observant home, scarcely even traditional. The Jewish content came primarily from Dad; he had attended *cheder* classes run by Gateshead's Orthodox Jewish community, had lived in Palestine for four years in the 1920s before his marriage and spoke fluent Hebrew as well as Yiddish. He could recite the prayers with ease and enjoyed going to *shul* and spending time with fellow Jews in the synagogue environment. He was an active member of the local Zionist movement, and with his command of Hebrew was called upon to welcome visitors, mainly fund-raisers, from the State of Israel. But he had lost his faith and, *shul*-going notwithstanding, paid little attention to Jewish practice. Add to this Mother's resolute atheism, and our isolation from the Jewish community during the war years when we lived in the country to escape the bombing, and it is clear why *kashrut* and Shabbat observance were not part of our way of life.

However, some bits and pieces did stay with us and I was never in doubt that we were a Jewish family. Pesach – first and second Seder nights – was lovingly observed, with family members who had "married out" and non-Jewish friends always invited, the Haggadah read from start to finish, and *matzah* on the table for the whole week. Chanukah candles were lit and gifts exchanged – but then we often had a Christmas tree and Christmas presents and went out carol singing. Mother's family was two generations ahead of Dad's. Her mother – my grandma Lena Jackson – and Lena's mother were born in England, old-timers in the country. They looked down on the newcomers from eastern Europe, who in their turn looked down on the refugees from Germany and Austria in the 1930s and 1940s.

My mother's contribution to our Jewish home came from the kitchen. Considering how un-Jewish she was in many ways, she had a splendid repertoire of Jewish dishes – *kuchen, gefilte fish, tzimmes, ptcha, knaidlach, latkes, borscht,* and of course the best chicken soup in the world – much appreciated by everyone, including our non-Jewish friends. And Dad fasted on Yom Kippur. That was about the sum total of our *Yiddishkeit*, plus Friday night dinners with candles and Palwin wine and Dad mumbling the *broches* (blessings). I didn't consciously reject any of this, but it was not central to my life, and it held no attraction for me. I grew up with little knowledge of or interest in Jewish history and customs, and a correspondingly deep love of British culture and tradition. Of Zagare and of Lithuania I knew nothing.

CHAPTER TWO
THE IRON CURTAIN

For people in the West, the Soviet Union was for more than seventy years out of sight, out of touch, out of bounds, somewhere out there in the East. The atlas showed a vast expanse of red, straddling Europe and Asia, one-sixth of the earth's surface. The various republics were not delineated and were simply exotic names from a past era – the Caucasus (Georgia, Armenia), the Baltics (Lithuania, Latvia, Estonia), Central Asia (Uzbekistan and all the other -stans). The Iron Curtain was a formidable barrier, and Jews in the West with family members still in the USSR were afraid to write letters to their relatives, let alone visit them. Under Stalin's totalitarian regime any attempt to make contact could place people on the other side in serious danger, and for decades families were condemned to remain split apart and out of touch. Few Soviet Jews managed to slip under the Iron Curtain and make their way to Europe, America or Israel. Even after Stalin's death in 1953 there was little change.

Following Israel's triumphant victory in the 1967 Six-Day War there was a revival of attempts by Soviet Jews to leave for the Jewish state. In the beginning a trickle of immigrants managed to make their way to the Promised Land, and the number of applications for exit permits increased dramatically in the 1970s. Some did get through, but most applicants were turned down, becoming refuseniks – Jews whose requests to emigrate had been rejected and who usually suffered severe reprisals.

I had made *aliyah* to Israel in 1960. There was no Zionist ideology behind my decision. Earlier in the year I had visited my sister who was on a gap-year volunteer program on Kibbutz Nir David, where she worked in the fields and also learned Hebrew. Israel attracted me, and with no family obligations to keep me in England, I quit my job at the BBC and decided to have a go at living and working in the Jewish state. I was fortunate to find work in the English Department of Israel Radio. In those years it was called Kol Zion Lagola, the Voice of Zion, broadcasting to the Jewish diaspora under the aegis of the Jewish Agency.

The years that followed my decision to settle in Israel changed me. My marriage, the birth of my children, and the experience of living in the Jewish state through the Six-Day War of 1967 and the Yom Kippur War of 1973 were transforming events. Living as an Israeli through those momentous times, together with my journalistic work at Israel Radio, put me in touch with my Jewish roots and opened my eyes and my heart to things Jewish.

It was in the year 1977 that I first set foot in the Soviet Union and had my first encounter with Russians and with refusenik Russian Jews. It was a period when the Kremlin was systematically putting down with an iron fist any manifestation of Jewish self-expression. Those who made the decision to apply for an exit permit condemned themselves and their families to an uncertain future in which they would face job loss, poverty, and the possibility of long-term exile and separation from loved ones.

My visit to the Soviet Union was, improbably, as a member of an Israeli delegation to the annual conference of the International

Journalists Ski Club. I say improbably because my skiing skills were practically nonexistent and in no way qualified me to be a member of any skiing team. However, there were very few skiing journalists to be found in Israel in the 1970s and to my surprise my application to join the team was accepted. I had learned the basics years before on skiing holidays in Norway and Austria, and before leaving Israel our team of journalists put in a few hours of practice on the slopes of Mount Hermon.

Israel was a paid-up member of the IJSC, and Foreign Ministry diplomats in Jerusalem were excited at the prospect of Israelis going to the USSR in an official capacity to take part in an international gathering. They supported us even to the extent of paying our airfares. When the Russians extended their invitation to host the annual meeting of the IJSC in Georgia, the offer was accepted on the understanding that all members would be welcomed and that all would receive visas. Initially there were objections raised to Israeli participation, but the IJSC stood firm and said they would cancel the conference if the Israelis were not allowed to participate. The 170 delegates from twenty-two countries came mainly from Europe, with East and West blocs represented in nearly equal numbers. One of the aims of the club was to promote "international understanding"; the presence of an Israeli delegation in the Soviet Union in the chilly atmosphere of the Cold War years was a source of much satisfaction.

Diplomatic relations between Israel and the Soviet Union had been broken off after the Six-Day War, and during this period were at an all-time low. Consular missions had been withdrawn from Jerusalem and Moscow, and we, the four team members – Werner Braun, a freelance photographer, Gil Kessary of *Ma'ariv*, Haim Tal of the ITIM News Agency and myself – had to present ourselves at the Soviet consulate in Geneva in order to receive our visas. We sat in silence in the ornate waiting room, assuming that there were microphones concealed in the chandeliers. I looked at the mirror above the rococo fireplace and wondered if we were being watched through a one-way window. This uncomfortable feeling of being followed and monitored stayed with us throughout our time in the Soviet Union.

Moscow's Sheremetyevo Airport was cold, noisy and chaotic; there were no luggage carousels, and suitcases and bags were brought on wagons by porters. It took a long time to get through passport control. A pale-faced youth in a green uniform and green peaked cap stared for a long time at each Israeli passport, lifted his cold blue eyes and stared at each Israeli face. Then we were waved on, and the Russian visit began. In Moscow we were wined and dined, taken to the Bolshoi Ballet and the Moscow Circus, and generally given the royal treatment. From there we flew to Tbilisi for sightseeing, more sumptuous meals, a dazzling performance by the Georgian Folklore Dancers, and then on to Bakuriani, a Georgian ski resort, for the skiing competitions.

This presumably was the Soviet Union's top resort, but the facilities were disappointing. Hotel accommodation and ski lifts were much inferior to those in Western Europe. Still we enjoyed our time there and were entertained by a visit from the chess grandmaster Gary Kasparov, who simultaneously played games of chess with twenty-four of the skiing journalists (including Haim) and demolished them all within ten minutes.

The real competitions, however, took place on the ski slopes – slalom, grand slalom and cross-country. Werner and Haim acquitted themselves well, but Gil and I were less successful. Still I was relieved to find myself not coming in last every time, but twenty-first out of twenty-two in the slalom and fifteenth out of sixteen in the cross-country. (OK, I was last in the grand slalom, taking nine minutes to negotiate all those curves, whereas the winner zipped through in one minute and thirty seconds. But what the heck, I did finish all the races, and there were plenty of non-finishers.)

Throughout the conference all the Russians we met – journalists, skiers, *politruks*, *apparatchiks* and hangers-on – treated us warmly and went out of their way to make the Israelis feel especially welcome. Then suddenly out of the blue, during the final general assembly meeting of the conference came an extraordinary, inexplicably hostile attack on the Israeli delegation, with clear overtones of anti-Semitism. We had brought with us from Jerusalem a letter of greeting to the IJSC from the head of the Israel Journalists' Association, inviting the ski club to hold next year's meeting in Israel. Haim read out this harmless message to the delegates, who received it with warm applause. Then came the diatribe. Daniil Kraminov, a senior official of the Soviet Journalists' Association, disdainfully rejected our fraternal greeting as "Zionist propaganda and publicity seeking." The Israelis, he thundered, were using the IJSC as a platform for their own nationalistic propaganda. The letter of greeting, he declared, should not have been read out; it should have been hand-delivered.

We were dumbfounded. Clearly there were political behind-the-scenes maneuverings of which we knew nothing. Two of us walked out of the meeting in protest, and two of us stayed to monitor developments. The warm atmosphere cooled. Some of the international journalists supported us, expressing their indignation at the attack, while others were indifferent and ignored it. We reflected on the workings of the Soviet establishment that welcomed us warmly with one hand and offered studied rudeness with the other. In the end we Israelis decided to play it cool. Throughout the remainder of our stay in Moscow and Bakuriani, we took even greater care not to speak of sensitive matters in our hotel rooms, which were surely bugged. Incidentally my address book went missing in Bakuriani, clearly lifted from my bag while

I was skiing. I complained and it was duly returned the next day.

However, the importance of our visit lay elsewhere. Our mission was to make contact with the Moscow Refusenik Scientists' Seminar, a group of leading Jewish scientists who were actively engaged in bringing their plight to the attention of international human rights organizations. In Jerusalem we had been given the address of Viktor Brailovsky, leader of the seminar, and were briefed about the refusenik movement. We were also warned to be discreet, to stick to the rules and not to give the Soviets any excuse to clap us into prison. On our second day in Moscow, Werner and I, armed with an out-of-date map of the city and speaking not a word of Russian between us, slipped away from our hotel and set out to find the Brailovsky apartment as instructed by our handlers in Jerusalem. And find it we did, in a dismal, shabby high-rise block. Viktor answered the door. "Viktor?" I queried. "*Da*," he replied. "We are from Israel," I said, in English. "Come in, I was expecting you," he answered calmly, and ushered us into the living room, whose walls and shelves were filled with Israeli memorabilia, maps, books and pictures. Clearly we were in the right place.

We met Viktor's wife, Irina, a mathematician, their son and daughter, and Irina's mother. By Russian standards their modest two-room apartment was a luxury dwelling in that the family had it to themselves. Viktor, a computer scientist and cyberneticist, had lost his job after applying to leave for Israel and now headed the Scientists' Seminar, which held weekly meetings in his home. We stayed only a short while, fearful that a prolonged absence from the group would arouse comment. We arranged to return after our skiing exploits in Georgia to lead a seminar for as many of the refusenik scientists as could come – to answer their questions and take messages with us back to Israel.

The following week we returned, together with Gil and

Haim, to find nearly twenty men and women crowded into the Brailovsky apartment waiting for us expectantly, the air charged with excitement and anticipation. It was as cheerful and lively a crowd as any we saw in Russia, and it was hard to believe that these men and women had ruined their careers by applying to leave for Israel. Some had been waiting for six years, unable to work in their professions, unemployed or doing menial jobs. The threat of arrest, detention, interrogation and imprisonment was always present. The effect on family life was dire; there were many with broken marriages and split families, and all were dealing with a multitude of problems – personal, social and economic.

The evening took off with an animated debate on which language to use. We the Israelis spoke no Russian, Yiddish was scarcely an option, and Yuli Kosharovsky, the dedicated teacher of Hebrew, declared in Hebrew at the top of his voice: "If we have Hebrew speakers in our midst then we must speak in Hebrew." But he was voted down and we settled on English as the lingua franca for the occasion. As the native English-speaker of our group I acted as moderator; I began by introducing my colleagues, ending with the words, "and I am Sara Manobla, radio broadcaster for the English Department of Kol Israel." There was a gasp from my listeners. "We know you," they cried. "We know your voice; we always try to tune into your shortwave broadcasts. And we know the voices from your Russian-language broadcasts." Someone added: "And we have many comments and criticisms to make of your broadcasts."

So began an intense evening of discussion, probing questions and frank comments on modern Israel. They were amazingly well informed on current Israeli affairs. There were questions about the upcoming elections, about the leaders of the political parties and the latest scandals, about higher education and university research departments, about the school system, and about housing and health care and other benefits offered to new immigrants.

Their passionate longing for Israel made me regret deeply the shortcomings and inadequacies of our country.

Yosef Begun, a leading dissident, was there, as were Vladimir Prestin and his brother-in-law Pavel Abramovich, the distinguished Professor Benjamin Levich, Alexander Lerner, Eliahu Essas, Benjamin Fein and Mark Azbel. They were all refuseniks of several years' standing, some of them leading scholars, highly regarded in their fields. Dismissed from their academic posts and deprived of research facilities, they now met regularly to discuss scientific developments, to give lectures, to maintain contact with their colleagues, to support one another in whatever way they could. Sometimes visiting scientists from abroad would take part in a seminar meeting. The dissident Russian scientist Andre Sakharov had recently addressed them and lent them his support. On a rare and happy occasion they would meet to say goodbye to a fortunate family that had received the longed-for exit visa.

It was midnight and time to go. There were notes and letters and messages to be carefully stashed in bags and wallets, for delivery to family and friends in Israel. And there was a plea that we were asked to pass on to Soviet Jewry activists the world over: "Things are getting worse every day," they told us. "There are more arrests. We face increased repression and harassment. The struggle for human rights is passing us by. Tell the Jews of the world. Please step up your protests. Do not forget us. We need your help, desperately." There were hugs and kisses, promises to stay in touch and the universal wish and Hebrew blessing *l'shanah haba'ah b'Yerushalayim* – next year in Jerusalem. Irina Brailovsky walked with us through the snowy streets to the Metro station. Yuli Kosharovsky traveled with us on the underground train and accompanied us to the door of our hotel, all the time speaking confidently in Hebrew and hanging on to our every word.

It was an evening that made an indelible impression on me

and led to my involvement in and long-term commitment to the struggle for Soviet Jewry. Soon after our return to Israel we heard that Yosef Begun, whom we had met in Moscow, had been arrested on charges of "parasitism" and was being held in a jail for serious criminal offenders. He was featured in a Russian TV film, *Traders of Souls*, and described as a Jew receiving financial support from Zionist organizations. Then came news of the arrest of Anatoly (Natan) Sharansky on charges of treason and espionage for the United States. The show trial that followed ended with his being sentenced to thirteen years hard labor in the Siberian gulag. There were several other high-profile trials of leading Jewish scientists and intellectuals, who were known collectively as Prisoners of Zion because of their desire to emigrate to Israel. We had paid little attention to the warnings we were given in Moscow of impending arrests and stepped-up harassment of refuseniks, judging them to be exaggerated, even hysterical. Now it was clear that the scientists' fears were well founded.

Back at work in Jerusalem I passed on to my colleagues in the Russian Department the many complaints, criticisms and suggestions about our broadcasts that had been voiced at the seminar meeting. They were mainly of the "the presenter of the so-and-so program is terrible; we can't understand him" variety, or "the political discussions are one-sided; let us have other points of view," and so on. But the chief complaint was the jamming by the Soviets of broadcasts from Israel, the deliberate transmission of noise on the same wavelength in order to interfere with reception in the Soviet Union. As well as the Russian-language service, broadcasts from Israel in Hebrew and Yiddish were also jammed, presumably on the grounds that they were aimed at a Jewish audience. There was nothing Israel could do about this other than bring the matter to the attention of international broadcasting bodies. At the general meeting of the IJSC in Bakuriani I had asked for permission to speak and had brought the issues of freedom of the airwaves and jamming of international shortwave broadcasts to the attention of my fellow journalists. My remarks were greeted with warm applause by the assembly and were recorded in the minutes. All this was just moments before Kraminov's anti-Semitic diatribe was directed at us.

English broadcasts were not being targeted, so Israel Radio's English-language service assumed a new importance as a means of reaching out to the isolated Jews of the Soviet Union, bringing them news and assuring them that they were not forgotten. My contribution was the inauguration of a weekly bulletin of reports on refusenik activities, which was broadcast in English on shortwave and heard by listeners throughout the Soviet Union. I established contact with a number of activist groups such as the 35s and the Public Council for Soviet Jewry, which kept me supplied with up-to-date information about the refuseniks and provided reports on the activities of protest groups in the West. "Let My People Go" was a regular feature of Israel Radio's English-language broadcasts for several years.

I tried to maintain contact with the Brailovsky family, but letters addressed to their Moscow apartment did not get through. Irina Brailovsky had asked me to get prescription glasses for her daughter, and I found someone traveling to Russia on a non-Israeli passport who was prepared to take the glasses to Moscow. But he could not deliver the parcel, and I was unable to keep in touch. Viktor's brother and father, who had managed to make their way to Israel some years before, kept up the struggle on behalf of the family. The news came that Viktor had been sentenced to exile, far from his family in the desert region of Kazakhstan, for publishing an underground magazine, *Jews in the USSR*. Things looked grim for the Brailovskys and for the other brave men and women I had met in their home.

Some years later, after finally being allowed to leave the Soviet Union, Viktor spoke about the Scientists' Seminar and his own arrest and exile in an interview with Aba Taratuta published in 2003:

> The authorities were afraid of it [the Scientists' Seminar] because of our contacts with the Western scientific community. They were apprehensive that their scientific and technological contacts with the West might be damaged. They realized that should the seminar be banned the consequences could be rather grave. Therefore, even when I was arrested in the '80s and they organized some kind of KGB siege blockade around my flat, the seminars were not banned. The seminar continued to function for a certain period, but then I was sent into exile and I suppose that one of the reasons for my exile was just that, my involvement with the seminar. My wife began visiting me at my place of exile, and thus the seminar had to leave our flat. The seminar traveled from one flat to another, and sometimes, when my wife was in Moscow, it was again held at our place. When I returned, the seminar was still traveling from place to place, but later, in 1984–85, it was fully revived. Besides having scientists visit us, we occasionally arranged international sessions; from fifteen to twenty scientists from all around the world would come to these sessions.*

In the mid-1980s a new era dawned, the Gorbachev period of *glasnost* and *perestroika*. Restrictions were gradually being relaxed and permission was granted to some of those who wished to leave for Israel. Russian could now be heard spoken in the streets and shops and buses of Israel as more immigrants began to arrive, though the numbers were still small. But there was no sign of the Brailovskys nor any word from them.

---

* Aba Taratuta, "Interview with Victor Brailovsky," Remember and Save Association, http://www.soviet-jews-exodus.com. Minor editorial alterations to the text have been made with permission of Viktor Brailovsky and the Remember and Save Association.

In 1986 I found myself once again on my way to Moscow, this time on holiday with three friends, hoping there would be another opportunity to meet the Brailovskys. I was on the last leg of a journey that had started in China, ending with a memorable ride on the Trans-Siberian Railway traveling east to west, from Beijing to Moscow via Manchuria and Novosibirsk, Irkutsk and Lake Baikal. On board the train, with my plan to contact the Brailovskys in mind, I had kept quiet about my Israeli/Jewish identity so as not to draw attention to myself. This time I was traveling on my British passport, but it was possible that the KGB had a file on me following our ski club visit in 1977. There was no way of knowing. Gorbachev and *perestroika* notwithstanding, the Soviet Union was still a harsh totalitarian environment. Our group of four was traveling independently, with no guide to help or interfere with our plans. Our visas for travel in the Soviet Union, obtained in Beijing, were valid for only nine days; this would cover the six-day train journey on the Trans-Siberian Railway, one day in Moscow, one day for the train journey out of the country and a spare day in case of delays. So there was a day in hand to get to the Brailovskys.

It was May, the sun was shining, the trees were in blossom, the air was sweet, people were smiling, and the ice cream at GUM, Moscow's main department store, was delicious – all very different from my previous visit. I phoned the Brailovsky number and Irina answered. Nine years ago their phone had been disconnected most of the time. Now we spoke, almost normally, and agreed to meet at the Metro station.

Their home was little changed. The children had grown; Viktor had returned from exile and had work of some kind. No, they had not received any of the letters I had sent them. They seemed discouraged and frustrated and told me there was little likelihood of their being allowed out. They were tired of the seemingly endless wait for permission to leave for Israel. I tried to encourage them:

"I'll be at the airport when you arrive in Israel," I promised them. "And we'll have a great party at my house with all our friends. I just hope it won't be another nine years till our next meeting. But we shall meet again, in Israel."

And yes! – a year later we were at the airport, bouquets of flowers at the ready, waiting to greet the Brailovsky family. Friends and colleagues from Moscow who had preceded them to Israel, members of Yiftach, the kibbutz that had adopted them, Soviet Jewry activists, and Viktor's brother, whom he had not seen for more than a decade, all gathered at Ben-Gurion Airport to celebrate the arrival of Viktor and Irina, their son Leonid with his wife and small son, their daughter Galia and Irina's elderly mother. As they came through the barrier we experienced a thrill of triumph and fulfillment. I embraced Viktor and reminded him of the promise I had made in Moscow. "I accept!" he cried with alacrity, and all that remained was to settle on a date for the reunion and send out invitations.

The evening at my house was no less noisy and lively than the Moscow gathering ten years before. There were activists from the Public Council for Soviet Jewry and from the Soviet Jewry Education and Information Center; broadcasters from Israel Radio's Russian and English services, whose voices were known to Viktor and Irina; former refuseniks, some of whom we had met at the Brailovsky apartment; and the four skiing journalists. We looked at photographs Werner had taken of that historic meeting; now he was once more flashing his camera to record this moment, the end, or perhaps only the beginning, of the Brailovsky story.

* * *

By the late 1980s most Jews applying to emigrate were being granted exit permits. The struggles of the refuseniks and the Soviet Scientists' Seminar were no longer relevant, already consigned to history. With the fall of the Iron Curtain and the end of the Cold War, immense changes were now sweeping through Europe. Religion was no longer proscribed in the Soviet Union, Hebrew could be taught in schools, synagogues and yeshivas were allowed to function. The always present latent anti-Semitism emerged into the open and reared its ugly head. Things were getting back to normal. As the breakup of the Soviet Union unfolded before our unbelieving eyes, the gates inched apart and then burst wide open before the torrent of Jewish emigrants leaving their homeland. The Russians are coming!

It was a landmark moment for Soviet Jewry, for Israel and for Jewish communities in other countries. In the early 1990s hundreds of thousands of Russians arrived in Israel and were given new-immigrant status with the accompanying privileges – accommodation in absorption centers or hostels, Hebrew language tuition, support classes for school children, tax relief, low-cost furniture and appliances.

According to *halachah* (Jewish religious law), many of the new arrivals were not actually Jewish. However, if they had at least one Jewish grandparent, they were eligible for citizenship under Israel's Law of Return. A non-Jewish spouse was also eligible. After seventy years of Communist rule when religious observance was banned, the Jewish community had lost its former homogeneity.

Not all the newcomers stayed in Israel, and after a period of acclimatization some began to explore the options open to them in other countries, in particular the United States, the *goldene medine*. At first the Americans gave refugee status to everyone arriving from the Soviet Union, but later initiated a system of quotas. Germany also was a favored destination for those seeking a better life, and the Germans offered many attractions for the new immigrant.

But it was in Israel that the effect of the huge emigration of the 1990s was felt most strongly. Over the years the immigrant Russians have made and continue to make a notable contribution in almost every sphere of life – political, economic, health care, social, educational, cultural, religious – though there have been many conflicts of interest and many disappointed expectations along the way.

My interest in the Jews of Russia was as strong as ever, now that they were here in our midst and becoming integrated into our society. I was particularly excited about the contribution they were making to the music scene in Israel. The music academies were revitalized by the influx of fine teachers and gifted students, the rank and file of the orchestras were strengthened by the string players who poured into the country, and the audiences for concerts of classical music and jazz increased correspondingly. It was said that a Russian Jew who stepped off the plane from Moscow without a violin case under his arm must be a pianist.

Soon Russian newspapers were being published; Israel Radio's Russian broadcasts, which had once targeted the Jews of the Soviet Union, became a channel for the newcomers, offering information and advice and providing a forum for airing disputes and queries. The Russian media outlets also heralded the entry of Russian immigrants into the political arena. Corner shops selling black bread, vodka, herring, pickled cucumbers and other staples opened in neighborhoods with large Russian immigrant populations. Shop signs and advertisements added a Russian text alongside the Hebrew. In 1991 a group of actors led by Yevgeny Arye moved to Israel and established a theater symbolically named Gesher, Hebrew for "bridge." From the start they attempted to work in both Russian and Hebrew, and over the years have made a significant contribution to the Israeli theater scene, a remarkable example of immigrant absorption.

The breakup of the Communist bloc sent shock waves around

the globe. It began in 1989 with the fall of the Communist government in Poland. Hungary followed suit. The climax came with the tearing down of the Berlin Wall and the subsequent reunification in 1990 of East and West Germany. Czechoslovakia was next. One by one the barriers came down across the Soviet Union, as the republics began agitating for independence: in Europe – Ukraine, Belarus, Lithuania, Latvia, Estonia; in Asia – Uzbekistan, Kazakhstan, Kyrgyzstan, Tajikistan; and in the Caucasus – a host of small republics of which we'd never heard. By December 1991 the Soviet Union had ceased to exist. Families long split apart could be reunited and there were many stories of Holocaust survivors and other displaced persons finding relatives lost to them for more than fifty years. Not only were people from the FSU (former Soviet Union) allowed to travel freely and even emigrate, but visitors from the West were at last permitted to enter and tour the countries of Eastern Europe without bureaucratic restrictions.

The shadow of the Holocaust often lay over these quests, with elderly survivors encountering people and places that brought back memories of the years of terror. Those looking to reclaim abandoned and confiscated property were met with suspicion and hostility. There were a few heartwarming stories of noble souls who had saved Jewish lives, but most were recollections of loss and suffering. Visitors to the old centers of Jewish life in the great cities of Europe were able to study archives and community records, decipher inscriptions on lichen-covered tombstones, and go back to the towns and villages where their families had lived. Jewish genealogy took a huge step forward, and a whole army of enthusiasts began to dig for roots, greatly aided by the new computer search technologies.

CHAPTER THREE

DISCOVERING ZAGARE

S ome years before, I had begun to look at my own family tree. There were no black Holocaust pages to grieve over, as Grandpa and his family had left eastern Europe before the end of the nineteenth century. I wanted to fill in the missing details but I didn't know what questions to ask, and in any case by this time there was no one left to answer them. Zagare and Lithuania were not yet in the picture. Only with the lifting of the Iron Curtain in 1991 did I realize that despite Grandpa's Russian passport, I was not of Russian descent. I discovered that I belonged to a family of Litvaks – Jews from Lithuania – but I still had no clue as to our place of origin.

The search for the family's Litvak roots was initiated by my non-Jewish cousins. Joy and Suki, the youngest of Grandpa's thirteen grandchildren, have always been close to my family. Their mother, my beautiful, clever Aunt Elsie, a concert pianist whom I loved dearly, was not Jewish, and the two girls were not raised as Jews. The Towb brothers, Uncle Louis (the handsome brother) and my father Willy (the clever brother), were close friends and our two families were much together. The Louis Towbs frequently came to us for Friday night dinner, and always for Seder night.

It was my cousin Joy who started to unravel the conundrum. Her father, my father's youngest brother, had outlived all but one of his siblings, and he was able to relate to his daughters the few memories of *der heim* that Grandpa Towb had passed on to him. The place names Kurland and Zagare found jotted on a piece of paper in Louis's desk rang a bell. Joy searched the atlas. She learned that Kurland, known also as Courland or Curonia, was a district formerly encompassing parts of northern Lithuania and southern Latvia. Zagare was a small Lithuanian town on the border between the two countries. But there was still no proof that this was our ancestral home.

A poster advertising a concert by the Lithuanian National Symphony Orchestra caught her eye. It was to be given that week in her hometown, a rare event as few visiting orchestras included Carlisle in their tours. Joy found the musicians in the concert hall about to begin a rehearsal. She approached them and without hesitation asked if there were any Jewish players in the orchestra. Someone pointed to the leader of the cello section and thus began her friendship with Valentinas Kaplunas. He heard her story and immediately encouraged her to visit Lithuania. "You must come," he said. "We have a beautiful country." With the bit between her teeth, with boundless energy and with very little knowledge, Joy decided the time had come to start looking for her family's roots. The hunt was on.

The year was 1995, barely four years since the collapse of the Soviet regime and Lithuania's declaration of independence. Travelers to the Baltic states were few and far between, and tourist facilities practically nonexistent. Joy cajoled her sister Suki into joining her, and it was their joint expedition to Lithuania that was the first step towards our accepting Zagare. The following account is based on the journal that Suki kept during that initial visit.

On the map Zagare looked close to the Latvian border, so my cousins flew to the Latvian capital, Riga. There they hired a car and drove south to their prebooked accommodation. The roads were very poor, their lodgings were somewhat dispiriting, and they nearly gave up on the whole enterprise. But after a night's sleep they set off for Zagare.

They arrived to find a small town, run-down, with little sign of activity. Traffic in the town consisted of horse-drawn carts and the occasional bicycle. It looked as though little had changed in Zagare in the past century. They made their way to the town hall. Joy had written to the mayor with details of their arrival; hopefully they would find someone to welcome them. No one was there. Disappointed, they decided to look for the one place they had to see – the place where the Jews of Zagare are buried. They found themselves at the site where on October 2, 1941, the Jewish population of Zagare had been massacred and buried in a mass grave. The grave, a long, narrow strip of land planted with flowering shrubs, is outside the town in a forest. It was marked by a bare concrete pillar and a few faded flowers.

Something had been achieved; they were in Zagare, the town Grandpa Towb had left a hundred years earlier. But there was a sense of anticlimax. They returned to the town hall. This time they found the secretary, who welcomed them but spoke no English. Then Zivile – an English teacher at the local high school – arrived, and things began to look up. A few minutes later Mayor Petras appeared and invited them to the only café in town. With Zivile acting as interpreter, Joy and Suki explained why they had come to Zagare.

Before leaving England, Suki had corresponded with a number of expatriate Lithuanians. Several people had warned against mentioning property owned by their family. Since independence this had become a matter of great sensitivity, and descendants seeking their Jewish roots might encounter suspicion and hostility. Joy and Suki decided they would say as little as possible about their ancestry.

Two days later, after some sightseeing in Riga, they returned to Zagare. Zivile and Mayor Petras were waiting for them, together with a sad-looking man who turned out to be the key to their whole adventure – Isaac Mendelssohn (in Lithuanian, Aizikas Mendelsonas), Zagare's only Jew, aged seventy-three, married to a Lithuanian non-Jew. He was to be their guide to this once-thriving town, where Jews had made up nearly 60 percent of the population. Together they went back to the mass grave. Mayor Petras had brought the three plaques that commemorated the massacre, inscribed in Lithuanian, Hebrew and Yiddish. They were kept in his office for safekeeping and put up only on the October anniversary when people came for a memorial gathering. The mayor and Isaac hung the plaques on the obelisk, and they all stood in silence, remembering. For Isaac visiting the site was always an affecting moment. His mother and sisters are buried here.

From the mass grave they visited the two Jewish cemeteries of the town. With Zivile translating, Isaac told them about his life and about the annihilation of the Zagare Jewish community. He invited them to his home, where his wife Aldona welcomed them. They found no family connection, but they worked out that Isaac's father would probably have known David Towb and his brothers. Where they had least expected it they had found a connection of sorts and had met the only person in Zagare whose family could have known the Towbs.

* * *

For the next fifteen years Zagare remained at the top of Joy's agenda, taking over much of her life, her energies and her time. On her return from Lithuania, she sorted out her notes, her diary and her photographs, and put together a talk with a slide show, which she presented to local groups. Her enthusiasm was contagious and she generated real interest in this little-known East European country, newly freed from the Soviet bloc. The impressions she conveyed of Zagare were of a community longing to be part of twentieth-century Europe, but immured in the past, and with few resources to propel itself towards a better way of life.

Clearly help was needed, and Joy rose to the challenge. The first hurdle she tackled was fund-raising. In her career as manager of an orchestra she had acquired a great deal of experience in organizing events, supervising budgets and – most importantly – in handling people. The small village where she lives, in the rural county of Cumbria on the edge of the Lake District in northern England, was hardly a central location for public activity. However, her home, Beech House, has a spacious barn that Joy and her husband had transformed into a concert hall and venue for events. It was a meeting place that had become well known in the district. It now became headquarters for the activities of the Friends of Zagare.

Joy had remained in close touch with Zivile, who advised the newly founded group on the needs of her community and how to direct their activities. Joy presented her talks, organized fund-raising coffee mornings, raffles and concerts, and began to collect stuff for the people of Zagare. A list of wanted items was sent out to people on Joy's mailing list. They were asked to donate warm clothing, fur coats (to wrap babies in), blankets, curtains, gardening tools, shovels, screwdrivers, nails and hammers, stationery, pens, pencils, notebooks, cutlery, kitchen equipment, walking sticks, crutches and books in English. A committee was formed and the group gave itself a name – Lithuania Link. In due course it became a registered charity, enabling it to apply to other agencies for support and guidance.

The first projects centered on sorting and packing the items collected from local friends and activists. In 1997 the first consignment of more than four tons of goods was sent to the people of Zagare, shipped in containers from Hull to Riga. A second consignment, similar to the first, sent a year later, included bicycles, sewing machines, computers, photographic equipment, toys, knitting wool and a vacuum cleaner, all secondhand. With money from sponsors and generous donations from individual supporters, Lithuania Link was able to award modest scholarships to two young adults from Zagare, one a teacher and the other an aspiring businessman. To direct and control all this voluntary activity an executive director was needed. Joy's neighbor, Alex Gibb, was only seventeen and had just finished his final school exams. He was inspired by meeting Joy and hearing about her visit to Zagare, and interested in her plans to build bridges with the newly independent country. Although he knew nothing about Lithuania, he rose to the challenge. Enthusiastically he took on the job of Lithuania Link director – unpaid – and over the next thirteen years proved to be a practical, efficient and resourceful administrator.

The Lithuania Link adventure was the start of a long and deep involvement for Alex as he began to acquire the skills and sensitivity needed to handle his partners in England and Lithuania. In the public sector he found a job as advisor to the European Parliament's president on matters concerning relations with Lithuania during the years prior to the country's accession to the European Union. In the private sector he joined in ventures to promote tourism and commercial development in several fields, and through Lithuania Link he became involved in a number of small NGO projects.

Being neither Jewish nor Lithuanian, Alex was well placed to take an objective look at the two peoples whose histories were so closely entwined and to examine the issues of racism, ethnicity, intolerance, acceptance and denial, keeping accounts and making amends. As he wrote to me some years later:

My involvement with Zagare through Lithuania Link was of a secular nature. Lithuania Link's ultimate objective from the start was to foster the roots of civil society to enable a person or entity to lead and be responsible for the non-governmental development of the town and its environs. Given the deep interwoven history of the Jews in the area it was clear early on that issues of race, gender, ethnicity and religion would all rear their heads sooner or later. We dealt with these issues during our work with the people of Zagare. As few immigrants live in the area, attitudes towards people of another race were less than tolerant; many men suffered from the decline of industry in the area following independence; women tended to hold the jobs and the families together while paternalistic attitudes reigned; the large Roma population in the town were actively discriminated against in verbal form by those in local government; negative stereotypes about Jews were alive and kicking despite the torrid past suffered in the very town. In the struggle to form a new national identity in post-independence Lithuania much of the inconvenient history has been sidestepped or rubbed out. The aims of our activities in Zagare were never focused on changing these attitudes and opinions. However, I feel that I learnt a great deal about the reasons, rationale and thoughts of our partners through our interaction, and have ultimately had a small hand in shaping them towards being more international and accepting.

After the initial project of collecting the goods and packing and dispatching the containers, Lithuania Link under Alex Gibb took off in new directions. Efforts were made to develop local industry and agriculture and to introduce tourism and modern technology. Local volunteer groups were organized, a youth club was established and projects initiated to encourage a revival of local crafts. Funds were raised for exchange scholarships, with young people from Zagare sent to study in England and their counterparts brought to work and teach in Zagare. In 1999 Alex founded the Zagare Youth Club, establishing links between Zagarean youth and the young people in his native Cumbria. He got together a group of youngsters to work alongside the Zagare Youth Club members on an environmental improvement scheme. He became fluent in Lithuanian and found himself very much at home living in the country.

Another of the Lithuania Link activists who settled in Lithuania was Sarah Rabagliati. She had come to the country intending to do a few months of volunteer work. In Vilnius she met Alex, who sent her off to Zagare as part of an EU-financed Lithuania Link project. There she worked on behalf of different elements in the community – the regional park, the youth club and the special needs school – staying on for two and a half years. Later she met and married Saulius Mitrike and in 2011 they returned to make their home in Zagare with their growing family. Although she is not Jewish, Sarah became involved in the Jewish heritage of Zagare and the Siauliai region. She collaborated on the restoration of the synagogues in Joniskis, a town not far from Zagare, and worked on a project to restore and document Zagare's Jewish cemeteries. Sarah was the inspiration and driving force behind the annual Zagare Cherry Festival, which since its inauguration in 2005 has become a fixture in the national calendar, attracting visitors from all over the world.

Apart from Joy, Cliff Marks was the only Lithuania Link activist whose ancestors originated in Zagare. An American town planner from Seattle, he came across the group by chance when he was doing a Google search for family roots. He was looking for information about his Zagare-born grandfather who had died in the United States when Cliff was a child. Cliff had now reached retirement age and was thinking about doing voluntary work. The Lithuania Link website with its Zagare outreach projects attracted him, and he was soon in touch with Joy. She invited him to come to Cumbria to attend a Lithuania Link committee meeting and decide how he might get involved. In Joy's house he had a long talk with Alex, who suggested that they meet in Zagare. Alex introduced him to people in the Joniskis municipality and later that year Cliff returned to spend six weeks in Joniskis working with local planners on their strategic planning effort. He prepared a report on the physical, social and economic conditions of the district and outlined the problems faced by the community. Together with Sarah he also became involved in the project to restore the two derelict synagogues in the heart of the town. In his spare time he taught English at the Zagare high school and led discussions on urban and environmental planning at Siauliai University. By this time Cliff was hooked. The following year he was back in Zagare, again working with Sarah, mainly on efforts to establish a small hostel in the town.

Joy's boundless energy and enthusiasm continued to inspire the members of Lithuania Link and fuel their activities. Herself a proficient instrumentalist (viola) and singer, it was natural that she would think of building yet another bridge, through music. Founder and leading member of the local Wordsworth Singers, Joy brought the choir to the 2006 Zagare Cherry Festival for a series of concerts. An outdoor concert of popular songs, light classics and folk music was held in Naryshkin Park and was attended by a large audience of all ages. On Sunday morning the choir joined local worshippers at the Old Church, where they performed a Mass specially written for the occasion by the Lithuanian composer Kristina Vasiliauskaite. In the afternoon they gave a concert in the New Church that included renderings of *Kaddish* by Ravel and *Kol Nidre* by Bloch. Joy went to much trouble to ensure that the printed program contained all the original texts with translations into Lithuanian. The music of the Wordsworth Singers reverberated and echoed beyond the walls of the church. Six months later the choir sang the same program in St. Mary's Church in Wigton, near Joy's home, with Kristina Vasiliauskaite in attendance for the Mass. The occasion was Holocaust Memorial Day.

* * *

Lithuania Link's second shipment was already on its way when I received the invitation. Zagare was planning a festive weekend to celebrate the eight hundredth anniversary of the town's founding and all Lithuania would be there. In appreciation of the help and support given to the people of Zagare by Lithuania Link, Joy and Alex together with their families, friends and fellow activists were invited to join in the festivities as guests of the town. Zivile and her fellow teachers at the Zagare high school would make arrangements for their stay over the weekend. Joy promptly began organizing plane tickets and car rental, and sent a note to her cousins and to Lithuania Link activists inviting us to join her party:

> A small group of friends and family is planning to go to Lithuania this summer for approximately one week at the end of June. The weekend of 27th–28th June 1998 marks the celebrations of the 800th anniversary of the founding of the town of Zagare, on the Latvian border, where Grandpa Towb came from. We also plan to see Vilnius, the capital, and go to the coast. This all follows the trip I made with Suki three years ago when we met up with various people there. Since then we've sent one load of aid and plan another to go out in May.

I was excited and signed on straightaway. I was also challenged. The prospect of setting foot in Lithuania brought home to me that I knew very little about our forefathers and nothing at all about our ancestral *shtetl*. In fact Joy and I were not entirely sure we'd found the right place. Regardless, we decided that Zagare would stand in for whatever town or village it was that Grandpa, Grandma and Uncle Jack had left behind in 1890 until such time as we were proved wrong. More troubling was the history of Lithuanian Jews in the twentieth century. By getting out in time, Grandpa had spared our family the horrors of the Holocaust. Nevertheless, the saga of persecution and suffering, of occupations and invasions – by the Tsarist Russians, by the Germans in World War I, by the Soviets, then by the Nazis in World War II and again by the Soviets, with a brief period of Lithuanian independence, each regime inflicting its vitriolic dose of anti-Semitism, discrimination, oppression, repression and finally genocide – was something I felt we all had to face before coming to Zagare. The Jewish story was not part of Lithuania Link's goal of reaching out to the people of Zagare. It was not on Joy's agenda, nor was it part of the agenda of the other members of her party.

Accompanying Joy were her husband Maynard; her daughter Jessica; Virginia, her cousin on her mother's side; Virginia's friend Bob; and the mother-and-daughter pair Ros and Esther, friends of Joy's. Later we were joined by Alex Gibb and his friends Mark and Jane, who came by car and ferry from England. Our group was Lithuania Link's delegation to the anniversary celebrations.

As the only Jewish member of our party, I clearly bore the responsibility for coming to grips with the history of Jewish Zagare. My knowledge of the period was at best sketchy so I made my way to the Hebrew University of Jerusalem on Mount Scopus. The library yielded plenty of material; I pored over a massive four-volume history written in Hebrew, *Yahadut Lita* (Lithuanian Jewry), and translated the chapter on Zagare, one of the more than two hundred communities documented therein. I added explanatory notes and put together a concise history of the community for Joy to distribute. This background research stood me in good stead when I reached Lithuania and had to deal with conflicting and contradictory accounts of the war years. My reading helped me to fill in the gaps and turned out to be a necessary and valuable learning experience.

I soon discovered that for the older generation of ethnic Lithuanians the past has not been put to rest. On the contrary it very much casts a shadow on the present, accompanied by much ambivalence, denial, guilt and hypocrisy. For those Lithuanian Jews who survived the Holocaust, remembering the past was a sure trigger for a resurgence of pain, grief and anger.

Trawling the net for sources and connections in Israel, I came across the name Len Yodaiken. Could this be Irish Lenny, my old friend from Kibbutz Kfar Hanassi? Indeed it was, though I had no idea that he was a *landsman*, a fellow Litvak, whose family, like mine, had come to Britain from Zagare. Lenny was the archivist, researcher and family historian for the Judeikin family, which before the war, going back many generations, had branches and family members living in Zagare and the surrounding *shtetlach*. He was very knowledgeable about Jewish genealogy and about Zagare. Our friendship was renewed, and he passed on much useful information from his own research and from his earlier visits to the Baltic states.

Lenny introduced me to www.JewishGen.org, the website devoted to Jewish genealogical research. I put in hours and hours at the computer trying to locate my antecedents and their place of origin. Truth be told, I never found any record of my ancestors, leading me to infer that in their day they had not left much of a mark on the pages of history. There was no indication of wealth or learning or distinguished lineage, what in Yiddish would be called *yichus*. The family tree that I had managed to draw up went back no further than the generation of the parents of Grandpa and Grandma, and the details of date and place of birth were incomplete. The trail had gone cold.

It took many years before new material came to light. In 2010 Joy visited Antwerp and together with Marijke van Wezer, a professional local genealogist, traced the family history of Grandpa's brothers from the time they left Zagare to settle in Belgium until the beginning of World War II. She even found and photographed the building that had once housed the Hotel Friedlander. We already had much of the information that Marijke unearthed in the Antwerp city archives, but it was gratifying to have official documentation noting that Grandma gave Zagare as her place of birth, that she and Grandpa were married in 1885 in Zagare, and that their eldest child, my Uncle Jack, was born in Zagare in 1886. So our claim to be of Zagarean descent was unequivocally confirmed.

Another of Lenny's suggestions was his recommendation of Rose Zwi's book *Last Walk in Naryshkin Park*, an account of the annihilation of Zagare's Jewish community, of the author's visit to the *shtetl* and her search for her family. I was enthralled and deeply moved by her superbly written account. In her narrative Rose Zwi combines her own research with her father's memories of his youth in Zagare. His guilt at having left his family behind in the *shtetl* and his failure to rescue his mother and siblings remained with Rose as she was growing up in Mexico and South Africa, and eventually in 1993 led her to Vilnius. There she met for the first time her Aunt Leah and her cousin Freda, who had survived the war years in Russia. Aunt Leah poured out her memories to Rose and these form the core of the book. With Freda's son at the wheel they drove to Zagare, and together they gazed upon the mass grave where their relatives were buried. And wept.

Carefully placed within the context of the broader scope of events unfolding in Lithuania, the Baltic states, Germany and the

Soviet Union, Rose Zwi's book gives a clear and detailed account of the fate of Zagarean Jewry, and it was my first introduction to the history of my ancestral *shtetl*. Usefully it also contains a detailed street map of Zagare, and I stuffed the book into my bag to take with me to Lithuania.

* * *

Zagare had been home to one of Lithuania's oldest Jewish communities, with a continuous presence from at least the sixteenth century until October 1941. In its heyday it was known as a city of Torah learning and wisdom. It produced famous scholars, writers and rabbis, the *chachmei Zhager*, the sages of Zhager (as Zagare was known in Yiddish), among them Rabbi Yisroel Salanter, the founder of the Mussar movement of Jewish ethics, and members of the Mandelstam family of writers and educators. There is an interesting perspective on the history of the community in the so-called *Big Green Book*, which was given to us by our hosts at the end of our stay in Zagare. A hefty tome, written in Lithuanian by local contributors, it was published in 1998 to mark Zagare's eight hundredth anniversary and covers every imaginable aspect of the town's life and history. I took the book back to Jerusalem to arrange to translate and study the chapter called "The Promised Land," an account of the Jewish inhabitants of Zagare as seen by their Lithuanian neighbors. The author notes:

> The first Jews arrived in Zagare in the sixteenth century, bringing with them their traditions and culture and their Yiddish language. The community was organized in the framework of a *kahal* which had its synagogue, cemetery, school, court of law and its own elective authority...headed by the rabbi. They did not mix with the Lithuanians and other Christians. Living in ghettos...they retained their ethnic character.

The writer goes on to list the trades and occupations that the Jews of Zagare were allowed to follow, different from those of the general population:

> They were generally goldsmiths, metalworkers, brewers, bakers, bookbinders, tailors, barbers, doctors, bathhouse attendants, musicians and traders.... The peasants were not allowed to brew vodka and beer, and it was licensed out to the Jews. There were twenty-six beer parlors and nineteen vodka parlors in New Zagare. Jews were licensed to rent inns and were allowed to collect market taxes as tax farmers.

The *Green Book* details the houses and businesses owned by Jews, the outbreaks of fire that destroyed Jewish property, and the cholera epidemic of 1848 in which 973 persons died.

For much of its history the Jewish community comprised a large proportion of Zagare's total population. In 1766, some 840 Jews lived in Zagare. By 1847 the number had grown to more than twenty-two hundred. The economic standing of the Zagare Jewish community was at its height at the turn of the century, with the Jewish population listed as 5,443 in 1897, some 60 percent of the town's total population. With the outbreak of war in 1914 the entire Jewish population of the town was sent into exile in Russia. Many did not return, and large numbers of those who did come back soon emigrated to the United States, South Africa or Palestine. The economy went into a decline from which it never recovered. In the period between the wars the Jewish population numbered around two thousand, falling to one thousand on the eve of World War II.

The outbreak of World War I found Lithuania's Jews caught between the two nations who were to dominate the history of the country in the twentieth century – Russia and Germany. Lithuania was still part of the Russian Empire when Germany declared war in 1914. The tsar's army, weak and ineffectual, was unable to repel the invading forces, and in 1915 Lithuania was occupied by the Germans. After more than a century of repression by the Russians, many Lithuanians responded enthusiastically to the German invasion of their country. However, the occupation ended soon enough, with the defeat of Germany in 1918 ushering in a new era. With the Russians gone and the invading Germans vanquished, Lithuania between the two world wars enjoyed a brief period of independence, and there was hope in the Jewish community for a better life.

In Zagare the economic situation was not good. The boundary between Lithuania and Latvia had been redrawn, leaving Zagare in an isolated backwater, cut off from markets in both Russia and Latvia. The Jewish population had dwindled. Nevertheless, the community was intact, remained optimistic and was still reasonably strong in trade and industry. The records show that in 1931, out of fifty-nine business premises in Zagare fifty-one were owned by Jews. There were synagogues, a Jewish old-age home, a hospital, two *mikvaot* (ritual bathhouses), two libraries – one Hebrew, one Yiddish – and two schools. There were Jewish sports clubs, Jewish youth movements, and even a Jewish fire brigade.

One of the positive outcomes of World War I had been growing international acceptance of the civil rights of ethnic minorities throughout the world. In 1919 the government of the newly independent Lithuania voted to introduce Jewish autonomy. This would provide for a Jewish Affairs Ministry and proportional representation in the government. Civil rights were guaranteed, including the right to use Yiddish in public and government institutions. It was a heady moment for the Jewish community. But the time between the two world wars was also a period of growing racism and xenophobia. Jewish autonomy in Lithuania lasted a bare seven years and accomplished little. Anti-Semitism surfaced once again.

In August 1939, one month before the start of World War II, Russia and Germany signed a non-aggression pact – the Molotov-Ribbentrop Treaty. In a secret protocol they partitioned eastern Europe into Russian and German "spheres of influence" with the three Baltic states – Lithuania, Latvia and Estonia – returned to the Soviet orbit. In June 1940 the Soviets began their invasion of Lithuania, occupying Vilnius alongside the Soviet share of Poland, as agreed upon in their treaty with Germany.

Lithuania, rapidly Sovietized, became the Lithuanian Soviet Socialist Republic. Russia, now the center of the Soviet Union, had always been feared and hated by the Jews for its repressive policies. But in the period following Hitler's rise to power and the promulgation in 1935 of the Nuremberg racial laws, the Soviet regime was viewed by the Jews of Lithuania as the lesser threat; for them Nazi Germany was more to be feared. However little they sympathized with the Bolsheviks, they derived a sense of security from the presence of Soviet troops on Lithuanian soil. For their part the Lithuanians disliked the Russians and did not conceal their hostility towards them. This divergence in attitudes towards the two warring invaders – one from the east, one from the west – has been and to this day remains a crucial element underlying and shaping Jewish-Lithuanian relations.

Then in June 1941 came Operation Barbarossa, Nazi Germany's surprise attack on the Soviet Union, an unanticipated rupture of the Molotov-Ribbentrop agreement. Lithuania, which bordered Germany, was the first of the Soviet republics to be invaded. Large numbers of Lithuanians welcomed the German invaders and were glad to see the hated Soviet regime come to an end. Public opinion by this time was almost entirely anti-Jewish. Jews were viewed as supporters of Communism, and as holding key positions in the

Soviet hierarchy. In *Vanishing Diaspora*, a survey of Europe's Jewish communities, historian Bernard Wasserstein notes:

> The revolutionary Jew [was] a source of right-wing paranoia and a stereotype of antisemitic propaganda.... Most Jews had not been revolutionaries and most revolutionaries had not been Jews. Yet the contribution of Jews to the revolutionary movement in Europe, both democratic socialist and communist, had been profound.*

Nazi policy towards the Jews was enthusiastically endorsed by many people throughout Lithuania. It was the prelude to the bloodbath that followed the implementation in the Baltic states of Hitler's Final Solution – the total elimination of the Jewish people. The Nazis were able to hand over to local militia forces much of the gruesome task of plundering and massacring the populations of entire towns and villages. Some 96 percent of Lithuania's Jews were murdered in the three years of the Nazi occupation, most of them within the months following the invasion. The remainder were herded into ghettos and used for slave labor until they were unable to work. This readiness of so many Lithuanians to collaborate with the Germans resulted in the almost complete annihilation of the indigenous Jewish population, heading the statistics of all the Nazi-occupied countries of Europe.

Following the German invasion of Lithuania, the day of reckoning for the Jews of Zagare was not long in coming. In June 1941 orders were given that Zagare Jews had to wear the yellow star on their clothing. They were forbidden to walk on the pavements, open the shutters of their homes, draw water from the wells, or buy food from local shops. In August the Jewish populations of

---

* Bernard Wasserstein, *Vanishing Diaspora: The Jews in Europe since 1945* (London: Penguin Books, 1997), 56–57.

several neighboring villages were brought to Zagare, where they were confined, together with the local Jews, in a district of the town that was fenced off with barbed wire. Len Yodaiken's family history contains a chilling account of the Zagare ghetto, as told by one of the few survivors, Bertha Taubman:

> On arrival we were greeted by a Lithuanian militiaman called Statkas. "You should have been shot like dogs a long time ago," he told us, "but if you behave yourselves and work hard, you will be given food. If you don't you will be shot." The partisans robbed, bullied and raped many. I remained there for ten days and most of the time I hid like the rest of the women.*

Bertha Taubman managed to get passes for herself and her daughter, and they were sent to the Siauliai ghetto just weeks before the Zagare massacre.

The story is taken up by Jacob Kagan, a native of the small village of Kriukai, not far from Zagare. He recounts how the Jews from his village and other nearby communities were brought to Zagare on wagons and herded into the synagogue in New Zagare, where they spent the night. Old and New Zagare were separated by the River Svete, and the ghetto was also divided into two parts. He estimates that about six thousand people were held there, most of them women and children. Many of the men had already been taken and killed. Those that remained were organized into work parties building fences to enclose the ghetto. At night they assembled for roll call and were sent to the synagogues to sleep. Women and children were separated from the men. At this time there were no Germans in the town. The ghetto was administered

---

* Testimony of Bertha Taubman, Yad Vashem Page of Testimony 8615086, cited in Len Yodaiken, *The Judeikins 1998: Family History and Tree* (Kibbutz Kfar Hanassi, 1998), 30–35.

by Statkas and other local Lithuanians, and there was no internal Jewish organization.

In September Statkas rounded up some forty strong men, saying they were needed for special work outside the town. They were taken to the Jewish cemetery in Old Zagare, where they were shot and buried in a mass grave. Kagan managed to hide. He writes that the strong young men were killed deliberately in order to preempt any resistance among the Jews in the massacre that was planned for the following month.

In the weeks that followed more Lithuanian militiamen were posted to Zagare. There were still no Germans to be seen. Then on the day before Yom Kippur the Einsatzgruppe A, a murder squad led by Commander Mantieff, one of the four SS special operations groups created to quash opposition in the newly invaded areas, arrived from Siauliai, where the German forces were based. The Jews were ordered to assemble in the town square and form into groups according to their occupations. Mantieff positioned himself on the balcony of a house overlooking the square. Kagan wrote in his eyewitness account:

> Suddenly Mantieff blew a whistle, and the murderers, who were concealed in the houses around the square, waiting for the signal, opened fire on us with machine guns. People fell over and died.*

There was an attempt at resistance led by Zagare resident Alter Zagorsky. Lithuanian partisans (who called themselves "freedom fighters" and had been active opponents of the Soviet occupiers) arrived to support the German soldiers and contain the uprising. More German forces were brought in from the Siauliai

---

* Yad Vashem Archives E1261 E/84.3.8, cited in Zwi, *Last Walk in Naryshkin Park*, 105.

headquarters. Jews who had escaped and gone into hiding were captured and brought by truck to the forest, where trenches had been readied. They were told to undress, and were then shot and thrown into the pit. Many were buried alive. Kagan wrote:

> By some miracle the bullets of the assassins did not find me. I was not hurt and managed to find a hiding place.... I was the only one who escaped from the Zagare ghetto.*

The day's happenings were documented in a memo sent to German army headquarters. It was drawn up by the commander of the Security Police in Kaunas, who noted that security police duties in Lithuania had been taken over by the Einsatzkommando on July 2, 1941. With customary Germanic thoroughness, the memo details all the executions carried out by the Einsatzgruppen forces in Area 3 during the first five months of the German occupation of Lithuania. Each town or village is listed with the date of the *Aktion* and the number of Jewish men, women and children killed. Starting with Kaunas, the killings continued, day after day, sometimes with more than one *Aktion* in a day. The commander of the Einsatzgruppe Area 3 squad was Karl Jaeger. He summed up the activities of his forces in a report dated December 1941:

> I can state today that the goal of solving the Jewish problem in Lithuania has been attained by Einsatzgruppe 3. There are no Jews in Lithuania anymore, except those needed for work and their families. Their numbers are 15,000 in Vilnius, 15,000 in Kaunas, and 4,500 in Siauliai.... The goal of ridding Lithuania of Jews could not have been achieved without the cooperation of the Lithuanian partisans and the respective civil offices.... Before

---

* Ibid., 106.

the Einsatzkommandos took over their security duties, it was primarily the Lithuanian partisans who killed the Jews.*

In some places a few Communists and Russians were mown down together with the Jews. The total for the period ending November 30 for the whole of Area 3 came to 99,084 persons.

The entry for the *Aktion* in Zagare, dated October 2, 1941, notes 633 men, 1,107 women, 496 children – a total of 2,236 Jews killed. A footnote adds: "As these Jews were being led away a mutiny rose, which was however immediately put down. 150 Jews were shot immediately, 7 partisans were wounded." The few survivors were those who had left the town before the German occupation, fleeing to Russia or hiding with people who gave them shelter. Thus Jewish Zagare came to an end.

---

* Jaeger report, cited in Masha Greenbaum, *The Jews of Lithuania: A History of a Remarkable Community, 1316–1945* (Jerusalem: Gefen Publishing House, 1995), 326–27.

CHAPTER FOUR
ZAGARE'S EIGHT HUNDREDTH

The story of Jewish Zagare was in my head and filled my notebook. Now came the reality of our visit there. June 1998. Our party of eight met in Vilnius and drove north in two rented cars, with mobile phones to keep us connected. We had arrived in Lithuania five days earlier and had acclimatized with some sightseeing in the capital and in the seaside town of Nida on the Curonian Spit. After reading Suki's description from only three years before, I had expected to find a depressed country, underdeveloped and backward after nearly half a century of Soviet rule. Instead I was surprised by the air of prosperity in Vilnius with its well-stocked shops and lively eating places. Intercity driving was easy on the excellent system of motorways, with even the secondary roads well maintained and well signposted. The countryside looked fertile and rich and well cultivated.

As we entered Zagare, Joy exclaimed "Goodness, how it's changed – all tidied up!" She attributed this to the celebrations that were taking place that weekend to mark the eight hundredth anniversary of the founding of the town. There were flags and banners and plenty of fresh white paint to smarten up the houses and public spaces. Alex Gibb and his two companions joined us in Zagare, making us a party of eleven.

We were greeted by Zivile, who was coordinating the arrangements for our stay in Zagare. A delightful young woman, outgoing, competent and practical, she took care of us for the duration of our visit. She led us to the school, where a splendid welcome feast was laid out in a grassy meadow surrounded by trees. There were huge quantities of wild strawberries, skewers of *shashlik* grilled on an open fire, rice, cheese on toast, washed down by beer, champagne and cherry brandy, all prepared and served by Zivile and her fellow teachers. There were schoolchildren who wanted to practice their English, and we were warmly welcomed by Mayor Petras.

The gathering lasted for nearly two hours. At last the guests were introduced to the hosts in whose homes we were to stay. As there was no hotel or B & B accommodation in the town, all the visitors were being lodged in private houses. People began to leave and I had not yet been placed. There seemed to be a problem and my would-be hosts could not be located. Perhaps, I thought, they don't want me.... Finally a solution was found and I was billeted in the famous Naryshkin Palace, once the home of the local noble family, now housing an orphanage and a residential institute for the mentally disabled. I was somewhat nervous about being on my own in this vast crumbling building and asked Jessica, Joy's daughter, to come with me. By then night had fallen, and the Zagare anniversary festivities were underway. Unfortunately it all seemed to be taking place in Naryshkin Park, right under our bedroom window, where a jazz band thumped along into the small hours. Many visitors from out of town filled the streets and the main square. There was a festive air of excitement in the town.

The next morning we assembled at the school, where the teachers had prepared a solid breakfast of hard-boiled eggs, rye bread, herring, cabbage salad and coffee. We then walked over to the town square, the center of Zagare, once the old marketplace of the town. Rose Zwi's book has a photograph of the square taken before World War II, showing it filled with peddlers, horse-drawn carts and stalls. Nearly all the shops and workshops there, which served the townsfolk and farmers from the surrounding villages, had been owned by Jews. Now it was planted with trees and grass and flowers; handcraft stalls had been set up for the festival, selling embroidered articles, amber jewelry and wickerwork. In the plaza, groups of folk singers and folk dancers were performing, dressed in local costume – embroidered aprons, lacy blouses and crocheted head caps. It all looked natural and unpretentious, laid-back even, and people seemed to be enjoying themselves. By chance Joy spotted Isaac Mendelssohn strolling by, and they had a happy reunion. I was introduced and we arranged to meet the next day.

The official part of the program got underway with eleven o'clock Mass, attended by the president of Lithuania, Valdas Adamkus. The approach to the church was lined with local children dressed in folk costumes, the girls with garlands of flowers in their hair and the boys wearing embroidered jackets and knee breeches. A band and uniformed guards escorted the priest and the guest of honor inside. The whole town was there, the church packed to capacity, the choir singing in the organ loft. There was an atmosphere of excitement and expectation. Compared to a similar event in Israel there was little in the way of security precautions to protect the president.

After lunch at the school canteen – yet another feast provided by the teachers – we walked to Naryshkin Park, the grounds of the former palace where Jess and I were lodged. The football field, a big grassy space surrounded by trees, had been taken over as the venue for the occasion. On a makeshift platform, groups of folk dancers were performing, young and old, some graceful, some clumping, all in folk costume. Canned music blared from the loudspeakers. After an hour of this the president arrived in procession, followed by local dignitaries, guards and attendants. The crowd of several thousand people filling the field began to push forward as the proceedings began. We, the invited guests from overseas, were ushered to seats in front of the crowd, next to the presidential party. Speeches, none of which we understood, were delivered by President Adamkus, Mayor Petras, the mayor of a city in Sweden twinned with Zagare, the local regional governor, and other notables. Then came Joy's big moment. Wearing a beautiful dress of flowing blue and green chiffon, clutching her handwritten speech, she mounted the platform. I was anxious for her, even fearful, as she addressed the crowd, but she exuded confidence and spoke into the microphone firmly and with conviction. Her voice was loud and clear:

> Ladies and Gentlemen: It is a very great pleasure and honor to be invited to Zagare for these celebrations, and we thank you for your warm welcome and your hospitality. I came here three years ago, with my sister, to find the town our grandfather left at the end of the last century. We were received most warmly then, but we were very disturbed to see the difficulties of everyday living many people have to endure in Zagare. I promised then that we would try to do something to help. Since then, Zivile and I have corresponded and our friendship has blossomed.
>
> You have a long and distinguished history. We are conscious of and remember the role the Jews played in the history of Zagare. They came here in the sixteenth century and helped the town to grow and prosper. And we remember too the tragic end of the community, in 1941, at the hands of the Nazis and their local collaborators. And we all feel very privileged to know Aizikas Mendelsonas. Our first meeting here was on a very cold day, early in May three years ago. It was truly a most moving experience.

It is time now for you to prosper again, and your English friends
would like, in a small way, to work with you, as equals. We can
assist each other, with a generous spirit, to a new understanding
and respect.

I was proud of my cousin. The previous night we had gone over
the text of her speech together. We decided that after "the tragic
end of the Zagare Jewish community in 1941 at the hands of the
Nazis" she would add the highly charged words "and their local
collaborators." She spoke of course in English, but her speech
was translated into Lithuanian and I was pretty sure I had heard
the word *collaborators*. How would the crowd react? Would they
boo her, stone her; perhaps there would be a riot, a pogrom? It
was no simple matter to stand up and speak about genocide and
collaboration to a crowd of Lithuanians. In the event nothing
happened. Probably nobody paid attention. I was relieved, but also
satisfied that the words had been spoken – to a crowd of thousands.

Joy's words were translated by twenty-two-year-old Valdas
Balciunas, a native of Zagare. A year later he was the recipient of a
Lithuania Link scholarship. He turned out to be a key figure in the
development of Lithuania Link and of our mutual efforts towards
reconciliation and acceptance of the other.

Next to speak was Alex – in Lithuanian! A triumph. I then
approached the president's aide. Presenting myself as an Israeli
journalist, I asked if I could have an interview with President
Adamkus. My request was granted, and I was asked to prepare
a list of my questions. The recently elected president was a fluent
English speaker, an émigré Lithuanian who had lived most of his
life in the United States, in exile during the Soviet years. On taking
office he had renounced his American citizenship, but promised
to bring modern Western thinking to the newly independent
Lithuania. Deliberately, my list of questions did not contain

anything provocative and we spoke at first about noncontroversial issues – agriculture, trade, ecology and the like.

When I asked him about the state of relations between Lithuania and Israel, President Adamkus answered my unasked question. He spoke at length about "the cloud that hangs over our two countries from the time of the Holocaust." I asked him about Lithuania's failure to put on trial war criminals and collaborators. He answered robustly that he was determined that "all those who were guilty of genocide will be brought to justice." "Even after fifty, sixty years have passed?" I insisted. He did not shrink from this. "Each man," asserted Lithuania's president, "has to be responsible for his own actions." His demeanor was sincere, even passionate.

I was duly impressed by his words and on my return to Jerusalem I broadcast my interview with President Adamkus on Israel radio. At a later date I had occasion to meet in Jerusalem with Ephraim Zuroff, director of the Wiesenthal Center, who has devoted his life to bringing Nazi war criminals to justice. He told me that since independence Lithuania had invested much effort in commemorating its vanished Jewish community with declarations and speeches, memorial plaques and monuments, support given to Jewish institutions, and similar gestures. All this he dismissed as nothing more than "window dressing" or "lip service." "To date no Lithuanian collaborators have been brought to justice," he told me. "More than half a century has passed, but Lithuania still has difficulty in facing up to its past." The undercurrents and ambivalences of Lithuanian-Jewish relations were becoming clearer and began to cast a shadow on the activities of Lithuania Link. The commitment of Joy and her fellow members to supporting the people of Zagare remained strong, but in the years that followed, they took a new direction.

From the assembly in Naryshkin Park we went back to the school for a workshop. Here we met key people from Zagare who were involved in health, education and environmental issues. The idea was to identify areas of need where Lithuania Link could be of help. My own feeling was that the need was no longer desperate, as perhaps it had been when Joy sent over the first of the "care packages." The town was not a flourishing community – the young people were leaving, there was unemployment, there were many old people and handicapped individuals in need of support – but it did not seem to be a site of dire misery and depression. Joy's enthusiasm notwithstanding, I myself was indifferent, even negative, untouched by the so-called needs of the town. From the very start of my involvement with Zagare, my interest had remained focused on the Jewish history of the community.

After our workshop there was a formal launching and presentation in the town hall of the *Big Green Book*, the historical survey of Zagare published to mark the eight hundredth anniversary. The copy given to our group was passed to me, with the hope that in Israel I would find someone to translate the chapter devoted to the Jewish community.

The day ended with supper at the school – *borscht, shashlik* and again heaps of strawberries – followed by the festival concert under the stars. All northern Lithuania had turned up for the festivities, thousands of people sitting on the hillside listening to the loud pop music and watching the fireworks. At midnight Jess and I trudged back to our palace and managed to get inside with some difficulty. The place seemed to be quite deserted. We had no idea where the residents had been sent. But at least the loud music was somewhere else, and we were able to sleep.

On our last day, we left the festivities and at last connected with Jewish Zagare. Isaac and Aldona Mendelssohn received us with warm hospitality in their small, modest apartment. Food and drink were set on the table. Isaac talked, almost robot-like, about the past, about his family, about the massacre in the square. But as he spoke of his mother and sisters he broke down. His eyes brimmed with tears and he left the room. Aldona took up the story. As a child she had witnessed the killing of the Jews in the town square and she shared her memories with us.

Rejoining us, Isaac then described how he had escaped the Nazis when they entered Zagare. A teenager, eager for action, he left the town on his bicycle, pedaling off the road whenever he saw the Germans approaching. He crossed the border into Latvia and headed for Riga. His mother had told him he would find relatives there. But the Germans had already arrived and he was not able to locate his people. In Riga he managed to get to the railway station and jump through the window of a train leaving for Moscow. En route the train was bombed and the passengers fled. Isaac ended up on a *kolkhoz*, a communal farm settlement. He had no money and nearly died of starvation. He sucked clover and ate berries for nourishment in order to survive. He decided to enlist and went on to serve in the Red Army for eight years, first in the Latvian Brigade and then in the Lithuanian Brigade. He was wounded twice. He unbuttoned his shirt and showed us the scars. "It still hurts" he told us, "especially in cold weather."

After the war Isaac returned to Zagare to learn that he was the only member of his family to have survived the October 2 massacre. A few other Jewish survivors returned to the town in those early days. All of them have since left. Why did Isaac stay? He shrugs and spreads his hands. "Where else could I go?" he says. "My mother and sisters are buried here." Isaac took over the task of tending the mass grave. Every year, on Yom Kippur, there used to be a *minyan* of Zagarean survivors. They would recite the Kaddish prayer for the dead and remember their loved ones. "Now" he says, "there is only me." Zivile is our interpreter throughout this exchange. I try to make conversation with my few words of Yiddish. Isaac knows no Hebrew. He is not a learned Jew.

With his broken nose, he has a boxer's face, a strong demeanor, proud and sad. "Are you not afraid?" I ask. He beckons me into the bedroom and opens the closet. Inside is a gun. "I am a hunter," he says, and with a knowing look he adds, "people don't mess with me."

Zagare's only Jew, Isaac was an icon in the town. There was little contact with the Jewish world. The rabbi in Riga would call to remind him that Pesach or Rosh Hashanah was approaching. Occasionally he used to go to Riga to pray in the synagogue. He would take the bus from the border or the rabbi would send a car. After Lithuania opened up following independence, Jews of Zagarean descent began to visit the town of their ancestors, as did Joy and Suki. They all made contact with Isaac. He and Aldona unfailingly offered them hospitality and told their story. We added our names to his list of visitors – a big sheet of yellow paper, signed by dozens of people from all over the world: America, England, South Africa, Australia, France, Israel – the scattered Zagare diaspora.

From Isaac's apartment, we went on to visit the three main sites where Zagare's Jews were laid to rest – the two cemeteries and the mass grave. On the way we found ourselves in the midst of a ceremony that was part of the anniversary celebrations. A large stone war memorial, prominently placed in the center of the town square, with the inscription "In memory of residents of Zagare who fell for their country" was being dedicated with official pomp and ceremony. Local dignitaries spoke, folk costumes and a military brass band were much in evidence, and an army choir of bemedaled soldiers sang rousing nationalist songs. It was a curious interlude falling between Isaac and the tombstones.

The weather turned gloomy. We followed the sign on the main road out of town directing us to the "Site of the Genocide of the Jews." The long strip of land planted with flowering shrubs that

▲ The Towb family, Swansea, 1903. Back row, *l-r*: Uncle Harry, Uncle Jack, Grandpa
David Towb; front row, *l-r*: my father William (in the petticoat!), Grandma Berthe (née
Moeller) Towb with Aunt Massie (Brodie) on her knee, Aunt Leah (Landau), Aunt
Becky-Rebecca (Landau). Uncle Louis, the youngest, was born in 1904.

◄ My parents William and Sylvia
(née Jacobs) Towb, silver wedding
anniversary, Newcastle, 1955

▼ Grandpa David Towb

▲ "Jewish Genocide" signpost to site of mass grave

▼ Mass grave and memorial obelisk

▲ Monument at mass grave: Joy Hall, Suki Pay and Isaac Mendelssohn, 1995

▼ Isaac Mendelssohn (with medals from service in the Red Army) and his wife Aldona, 1997

▲ Zagare synagogue

▼ Naryshkin Palace

Joy Hall addresses the eight hundredth anniversary gathering, 1998. *Left*, Valdas Balciunas translating; *right*, Alex Gibb ➤

➤ Sara Manobla interviewing Lithuanian President Valdas Adamkus at anniversary gathering

▲ Folk dancers in town square, anniversary celebrations

▼ Teachers at Zagare high school read from *Last Walk in Naryshkin Park* by Rose Zwi

▲ Ruth Yoffe, Holocaust survivor, Jerusalem, 2012

▼ Ruth Yoffe as a child

▼ Juozas Petrulis, leader of a group of Tolstoyans who saved many Jews

▲ The Levinskas home, where Ruth and her grandmother were hidden

◄ Leonas and Zofija Levinskas
at the front door of the family home

Leonas Levinskas shows Rose, ➤
Rod and Valdas his archive

Lithuanian newspaper article ➤
about the Tolstoyans, with
picture of Edvardas Levinskas

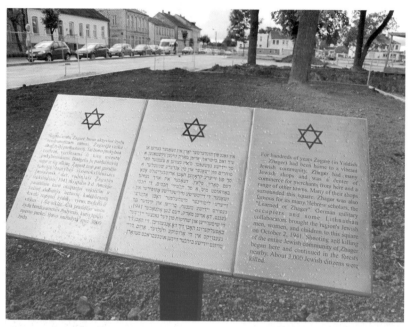

▲ Memorial plaque in Zagare town square

▼ Litvaks and Lithuanians attend the dedication ceremony, Zagare town square, 2012

▲ Rose Zwi unveiling the plaque as Dovid Katz recites Kaddish, Rod Freedman at left

▲ House of Pots and Pans

▼ Musical instruments from Leib's band

▲ Shabbat gathering; Zagarean descendants celebrating. *L-r*: Rod Freedman, Cliff Marks, Hazel Woolfson, Leonora Vasiliauskiene, Joy Hall, Sara Manobla, Rose Zwi, Raymond Woolfson

▼ Joy Hall

▼ Valdas Balciunas

▲ Righteous among the Nations award, 2013. Leonas Levinskas speaks; Valdas translates

◀ Leonas Levinskas receiving medal and certificate

19/03/2013

▲ Zagare Old Cemetery

▼ Monument to forty Jewish men murdered in 1941 and buried in the Old Cemetery

▼ Could this be the grave of my great-grandfather? Inscription reads: Reb Ze'ev Wolf, son of Reb Yitzhak Moeller

▲ Zagare under snow, March 2013

Joy and Suki had seen three years earlier was unchanged. But the obelisk now had a triple plaque permanently riveted onto its concrete surface. The inscriptions in Hebrew, Yiddish and Lithuanian commemorated "the three thousand Jews who in 1941 were killed by the Hitlerist murderers and their local helpers." Three years ago, the wording on the removable plaque that Mayor Petras had propped up for Joy and Suki to see made mention of "three thousand Soviet victims of the fascist murderers...." So perhaps attitudes were changing, as Adamkus had indicated, with some recognition of the particular suffering of the Jews. Or perhaps, in Zuroff's words, it was merely window dressing. Clearly the three thousand murdered Jews were not included in the "residents of Zagare who fell for their country," who were being honored that day in the town square. We stood there in the wind and rain, lost in thought. A somber moment.

From the mass grave we went to the town's Jewish cemeteries. At the entrance to one of them is a plaque commemorating the forty Jewish men who were rounded up just before the massacre, brought to the site and killed on that very spot. Both the graveyards were overgrown and neglected. There is no one left to take care of them. Most of the headstones were difficult to decipher, toppled over and lichen covered. Everything was overrun with grass and weeds, but there were no signs of vandalism or desecration. I took some photographs and when they were developed and printed I was able to read the Hebrew inscriptions more easily. One of them read "Reb Ze'ev Wolf, son of Reb Yitzhak Muller." Could it be that I had found the grave of an ancestor? My paternal grandmother, Grandpa Towb's wife, was born in Zagare, and her name was Batya Muller (or Moeller or Miller). The Hebrew name of her third son, my father, was Ze'ev, and Ze'ev is the name of my firstborn. The names and the dates all seemed to add up but there was no proof. Despite hours of trawling the JewishGen website, and a professional search conducted by genealogist Len Yodaiken, no evidence has yet come to light.

On our last morning in Zagare we were back in the school for breakfast. I still had *Last Walk in Naryshkin Park* in my bag and I showed it to Aldona Bagdoniene, one of the English teachers, a colleague of Zivile. She sat down, started to read, and then called over her fellow teachers. She began reading aloud from the book, translating into Lithuanian. All of them listened intently, fascinated, and the reading continued for some time. Aldona said she would like to use the text for her English lessons. I told her she could keep the book and I would send her some more copies. The women had welcomed us with unstinting generosity and consideration, and it was hard to know how to thank them. We took our leave with hugs and kisses and promises to stay in touch.

Placing my copy of *Last Walk in Naryshkin Park* in Aldona's hands was a catalyst that pushed the Zagare story in new directions. Aldona kept her promise and went on to use the book in the classroom as a study text for her English lessons. She told Alex Gibb that she couldn't bear to read some of it "because it was so awful." Yes, she did know that terrible things had happened in Zagare, but she had not known that it was the Lithuanians who had done so much of the dirty work.

Rose Zwi's book, painstakingly researched, had made a deep impression on me. *Last Walk in Naryshkin Park* is beautifully written in sparse, elegant prose, with a wry humor and an underlying passion that gives power and depth to the narrative. The dialogue sparkles, peppered with Yiddishisms, as the author relentlessly questions her interlocutors. On my return home I contacted Rose Zwi through her publishers in Australia and sent her an account of Aldona using her book in the classroom. With my letter I enclosed the photograph I had taken of Aldona reading aloud from the book to her fellow teachers. This was her response:

> **Rose to Sara:** I was very moved by your email. Could I ever have imagined when I set out to write the book that it would one day find its way into a school in Zagare? What a dramatic way of returning "home." It was indeed courageous of Aldona to have introduced it to her students. I'm sure it wasn't easy. But at least it might plant a seed, create a few ripples, make an occasional student think about the Unspeakable. If for no other reason than that the book is out, accessible, with the possibility of keeping the subject alive, especially in Zagare, I feel rewarded for the years I've spent on it. It's the best prize one could get for a book. The curtain has been lifted a few centimetres on some unacknowledged guilt that is eating away at the heart of a community. If only they could say – yes, it happened, it was terrible, it must never happen again.... If only I had met Aldona when I was desperately trying to make contact with people in Zagare and not knowing where to begin. It is heartening to know that people like Aldona exist.

Aldona was asked by Isaac and Aldona Mendelssohn to translate passages in *Last Walk in Naryshkin Park* concerning them and other people they knew. Some of the pupils also tried their hands at translating from the book. Rose and her publishers in Australia, the Spinifex Press, together with members of Lithuania Link, attempted to promote the project and get the translation published. Then problems surfaced:

> **Joy to Sara:** Aldona seems to be getting stuck with translating the book. She is talking about improving the text that they have already translated into Lithuanian, i.e., not continuing with the highly sensitive chapters where collaborators are named. What do you do? It's not straightforward, is it?

Aldona eventually wrote about the problems she had encountered. The translation project added a lot of extra work to her already overloaded timetable. The text was difficult, and in addition she and the students were not familiar with the Jewish background.

> **Aldona to Rose:** They found it too literary, especially the Yiddish songs and poems, which we were unable to translate. But the main reason we stopped using it was that some Zagare residents did not like the "bad light" in which you had portrayed the Lithuanians. I was advised by friends to stop the translation.

In the end Aldona dropped the project. It was disappointing, but none of us were surprised at the turn of events.

From here my friendship with Rose developed and we corresponded regularly by e-mail, finding that we had much in common. Finally in 1999 I met her and her husband, Wolf, when they came to Israel for a visit. After leaving South Africa and before settling in Australia, they had lived in Israel for three years. Rose had done research for her book in Israel and still had many connections with the country. During their visit we got together several times and Rose also visited my friend Lenny Yodaiken, historian of Jewish Zagare. One of the aims of her visit was to promote her book, which had been published the year before. I introduced her to people I thought might be able to help and wrote a review of the book for the *Jerusalem Post*:

> Naryshkin Park is a meadow on the outskirts of the little town of Zagare, where children once played on the grass and lovers strolled under the trees. In 1941 it became a killing field. The entire Jewish community, murdered by the Nazis and the local partisans, was interred here in a mass grave. Rose Zwi's father had left Lithuania in 1927, promising to make his fortune and send for his widowed mother and his siblings. But it wasn't to be. Born in Mexico, Rose grew up in South Africa, her parents burdened by grief and guilt, with questions unasked and unanswered. Her father never forgave himself for his failure to rescue his family

from the Holocaust. His daughter writes: "he died of a broken heart, misdiagnosed as a coronary."

The book tells the story of her journey to the past, of her meetings with Zagare "landsmen" now living in Israel, South Africa and the United States, of her research into the Yad Vashem and YIVO archives. She gives a bittersweet account of the lives of her parents in *der heim*, and of her own childhood in Johannesburg. When she finally made the journey to Vilnius, she discovered there her Aunt Leah, a stoic survivor of the Holocaust, now remarried and with a new family of her own. Together the two women journeyed to Zagare.… They visited the mass grave where their relatives were buried, they looked at the houses where their ancestors had lived, they scanned the sullen faces of the townspeople and wondered what role they had played in the massacre of their Jewish neighbors. The central figure of her book is her father's brother, her Uncle Leib, Aunt Leah's first husband – town barber, musician and revolutionary, and finally soldier, who was killed fighting the Germans.

Her search is dominated by the question "How could people who had lived side by side for generations turn on their neighbours or stand by as they were being massacred?" The acknowledgment she needs is not forthcoming, and she leaves Zagare with the question still unanswered.

Although the efforts to have it translated into Lithuanian came to nothing, *Last Walk in Naryshkin Park* has been translated into other languages and is a classic narrative of the Holocaust. The book came to the attention of Valdas Balciunas, the young Lithuanian who translated Joy's speech at the eight hundredth anniversary celebrations. As a schoolboy he had studied English in Aldona's class. Following Alex's recommendation Valdas was granted a Lithuania Link scholarship, the first to be awarded by the group. In 1999 he flew to England, for a brief, intensive study program. It was the first time he had ever been out of Lithuania. Joy and other Lithuania Link members were there to take him by the hand and introduce him to the English way of life. He spent a few days with Joy and her family. One evening Joy put Rose Zwi's book into his hand. It changed his life. When he finished reading it he wrote to the author:

> **Valdas to Rose:** May I please introduce myself and say a little about the circumstances in which I write. My name is Valdas Balciunas, I am 22 years old, and I was born in the little town of Zagare. Last summer, when our town was celebrating its 800th anniversary, I met Joy and her family and friends. An opportunity then arose to visit the UK to study. Whilst staying at Joy's in Cumbria I read your book *Last Walk in Naryshkin Park*, which has moved and appalled me more than I can say. I did know what happened in 1941 in Zagare, but I want to say to you how full of pain and sorrow I am on behalf of my community. I do share it, and am continually aware of the tragedy. There are people who remember and care about what happened – and these memories and truths are a part of my own and future generations.

> **Rose to Joy:** Please thank Valdas (I haven't his letter with me) for his very touching letter. It's something I've been wanting to hear from someone in Zagare, or from anyone in Lithuania for that matter, and he's helped restore my faith in humanity. Explain that I'm too distressed at the moment to write to him personally. He sounds like a lovely person and I hope we'll meet one day.

From this point on Valdas's interest in the history of the Jews of his country and of his own hometown grew ever stronger. He determined to do what he could to find ways of bringing young people of his generation to learn and face the truths of history and to come to terms with the role played by the generation of his grandparents in exterminating the Jews of Lithuania. He remained in close touch with Alex and Joy and played a leading role in developing and promoting the projects of Lithuania Link.

The group, led by Joy and Alex, continued its work. Over the years, Joy kept me up to date on her visits to Zagare and on the activities of Lithuania Link. I confess that I was less than supportive of her "Lady Bountiful" efforts – indifferent at best, even hostile. But, amicably, we agreed to differ. Seven years after my first visit to Zagare, I had written:

> **Sara to Joy:** The goals and projects of Lithuania Link are indeed admirable, but they are not part of the Jewish agenda. Enhancing the life of the town, making friends, social projects and planting cherry trees are absolutely fine, and many people might wish to support these. But in Zagare itself, with its one remaining Jew, there is little to indicate any coming to terms with the past. The project to translate *Last Walk in Naryshkin Park* foundered, apparently because of political pressure on the teacher. There has been no attempt to restore any of the remaining Jewish buildings there. The *mikve* is used as a swimming pool, the two synagogues are storehouses. To the best of my knowledge there is no plaque or memorial in Zagare other than the monument at the site of the mass grave and the plaque at the entrance to the cemetery. What news of Isaac? His presence in Zagare and that connection with the past is the only thing in Zagare that means anything to me.

> **Joy to Sara:** Lithuania Link is a secular charity, working to aid a ravaged town to come to terms with its past, bridging the divide between cultures, making friends, encouraging respect without forgetting history. Such things are necessary. Without it the world would be a very bleak place. Dear cousin, you may think it's pie in the sky and I'm wasting my time. But confrontation is not the way forward – it turns people away.

Understanding took time, but I was beginning to come closer to Joy, and she, I think, to me. The next ten years was a period of change and rethinking for many of us. It led to the demise of Lithuania Link, of natural causes, as Zagare inched its way out of the slough of despond and into the twenty-first century. As his career advanced it was no longer practicable for Alex to continue in his role as executive director. Without his help the program of activities in faraway Zagare could not be managed effectively. A new voluntary organization, wholly Lithuanian, with objectives similar to those of Lithuania Link, took over its assets. Joy, Cliff, Sarah, Alex and Valdas remained in contact. In the wake of the projects initiated by Cliff and Sarah and others, the Jewish issues and the Jewish history of the town came to the fore and assumed a greater importance.

* * *

Our visit to Lithuania in 1998 had ended with a few days in Vilnius, known to Jews of a bygone era as Vilna – *Yerushalayim d'Lita*, Jerusalem of Lithuania. Our guide for a tour of the city was Roza Bieliauskiene, fluent in Yiddish, English, Russian and Lithuanian, and with some knowledge of Hebrew. She was born in Vilnius in 1946 and had lived there all her life. Her parents had fled to the Soviet Union before the Nazi occupation, returning after the war to their home in the Jewish Quarter of Vilnius.

The central part of the city was a delight, with its broad, tree-lined boulevards and handsome buildings, shops stocked with luxury goods and a general air of prosperity. People were smartly dressed, the women tottering over the cobblestones in expensive high-heeled shoes, the men in impeccable suits. There was nothing that recalled the Soviet era. Little English was to be seen on signs and menus, so presumably there were few Western tourists in town. The Old Town reminded me of Prague – the light-hearted, flamboyant architecture with decorative carvings, the profusion of baroque churches, the fine restoration work being done everywhere. Pilies Street was a rainbow of pastel-washed plaster walls – lemon, peach, pale green, blue-gray – lending color and charm to the narrow, winding streets. The public spaces were being planted with gardens and the asphalt pavements replaced with brick tiles.

Roza had originally trained as an engineer, but reaching out to her Jewish heritage had brought her into the Jewish cultural academic world. She began to teach Yiddish, learned from her parents as a child, and now had a position as a curator at the Vilnius Jewish Museum. She also worked as a guide, and translated and did archival research for Litvaks from other countries who were searching for their roots. She took us first on the general tourist route, telling us about Gedeminas and the other dukes of Vilnius, about paganism in the Baltics and about the birth of Christianity. It was somewhat routine. Only when we reached the Jewish Quarter did she come to life, getting into her stride and capturing our attention. Our party had been joined by Valentinos Kaplunas, the Jewish cellist with the Lithuanian National Symphony Orchestra, who had been the first to encourage Joy to visit the land of her forefathers.

Roza took us into the old ghetto, where we walked along Zydu gatve, the Street of the Jews, a row of small single-storey houses, with windows overlooking the pavement. Here the Jewish merchants used to display their goods and do business with the passersby. Everywhere there were plaques, recently put up by the government, marking the places where the Jews of Vilnius had lived, where they had been confined, rounded up and slaughtered in the 1940s. The inscriptions were usually in Lithuanian and Yiddish. We looked at the statue of Rabbi Elijah, the Gaon of Vilna, the great eighteenth-century Jewish scholar and Talmudist, who turned Vilna into the foremost center of Jewish learning. The statue, with the inevitable explanatory plaque, had been erected near the house where he had lived. His remains had been reburied some years ago, in the Soviet period, when the old Jewish cemetery was demolished and taken over for public housing.

My thoughts returned to the words President Adamkus had spoken to me earlier that week in Zagare. Was all this part of Lithuania's determination to accept and acknowledge the past? Or could it more accurately be described as cynical lip service and window dressing, an attempt to ingratiate Lithuania with the international community? Roza spoke at length about the period of the Nazi occupation of the city and the Vilna ghetto. She told us about Jacob Gens, the controversial figure who headed the *Judenrat*, the Jewish council of Vilna, and his dealings with the Nazis. We entered courtyards where Jews had lived, imagined the scenes of the *Aktion* roundups, the suffering, the misery. We saw the sites of former synagogues and looked at buildings that had housed the Jewish hospital, Jewish schools and a Jewish library. Plaques were everywhere on the walls. In the area of the old ghetto we were joined by Joy's Lithuanian friends Daiva and Kristina, in whose apartment some of our group were staying. The window of their living room overlooked the courtyard of the former Jewish hospital, but they were not aware of the events that had taken place there. Daiva and Kristina were hearing for the first time about the history of the Nazi terror in their own city.

After the guided tour I found time to explore Vilnius on my own and visit the Jewish Museum, devoted to the history of Lithuanian Jewry, known as the Green House. No window dressing here, no need for plaques. An intense and moving narrative unfolds, telling the story of more than two hundred Jewish communities across Lithuania and their annihilation under the Nazi regime. The place is simple and unpretentious. Compared to sites such as the Anne Frank House in Amsterdam or the Jewish Quarter of Prague, there was very little activity and few visitors. I was shown a model of a grand new building that one day will replace the Green House, but fifteen years after my visit there, no progress had been made.

A few blocks down from the Green House is the Vilnius Choral

Synagogue. Before the Nazi and Soviet occupations, Vilnius had over two hundred synagogues and prayer houses, serving a Jewish population of about a hundred thousand, some 45 percent of the total population of the city. During the war the building was used as a storehouse, so it remained standing. The other synagogues were destroyed. Today services are held at the Choral Synagogue for the few thousand Jews who live in Vilnius.

As I gazed at the fine façade of the building, I noticed some men standing at the entrance steps during a break in the prayers. I approached them and introduced myself as a visitor from Jerusalem. "Yiddish?" they queried, and looked at me with suspicion when I shook my head. I said hopefully, "*Ivrit* – Hebrew?" Finally someone called over an elderly man who spoke a fluent Hebrew, with modern pronunciation and an extensive vocabulary. I asked him why he had not made the move to Israel. With his excellent command of Hebrew he would surely be able to settle without difficulty. He told me that he had a mission – to keep Jewish learning and culture alive in Vilnius. As a teacher of Hebrew he prepared young boys for *bar mitzvah* and was called upon to read from the Torah and lead the prayers. "Have you visited Israel?" I asked. "Several times," he replied. "My son lives there." And he added proudly, "He works in Israel Radio, in the Russian Department." "I too work in Israel Radio, in the English Department," I told him. It turned out that his son was a colleague I had known for many years.

Further along Pylimo Road is the Jewish Community Center, which houses the other part of the Jewish Museum, devoted to Jewish culture and tradition. Roza had her office there and she had invited me to drop in and see the exhibitions on display – relics from the Great Synagogue, a room devoted to the Righteous among the Nations and a display of paintings by a young local artist, Solomon Teitelbaum. We had lunch together and Roza told me about her son Julius, who was a student at the Hebrew University and living in Jerusalem. Would I take a letter for him, with some money enclosed?

My meeting with Julius upon my return to Jerusalem and our subsequent friendship led to a whole new chapter in my search for my Litvak roots and my return to Zagare. After telling him about my trip to Lithuania and handing over his mother's letter, I asked Julius if he could help me with translating some material written in Lithuanian. He agreed readily, and we sat down together to tackle the "Promised Land" chapter in the *Big Green Book*.

Lithuanian was Julius's mother tongue. He had come to Israel the previous year and his knowledge of Hebrew was still limited. His English was fluent but not always accurate. We worked in tandem: Julius gave me the gist of the text, either in English or in Hebrew, we discussed the unclear passages and I then typed it all out in acceptable English. We needed several sessions to complete the work, and Julius would usually stay for a meal. I learned that he was very much on his own in Jerusalem, with no family to turn to and few resources.

This was the period of mass immigration to Israel from the former Soviet Union, and there were many young students from Russia at the Hebrew University. They were granted certain privileges regarding language, such as permission to take exams in Russian. Most of the young Jewish immigrants from Lithuania belonged to Russian-speaking families and Russian was their first language. Julius, however, came from a Lithuanian-speaking Jewish family. He told me that there was little social interaction between the two groups. Of course he knew and spoke Russian, but his first language was Lithuanian. In Jerusalem there was no one with whom he could comfortably talk in his native tongue. But he had no complaints. I was impressed by his determination to make a success of his stay in Israel and by his general optimism.

His genuine interest in our Zagare story and in the *Big Green Book* made our translation work a pleasure and added to my knowledge and understanding of the Lithuanian Jewish community and its history.

As it happened, the small apartment attached to my house was unoccupied at the time. I offered it to Julius and he came to live with us. Soon he was very much part of my family, and he stayed on for nearly five years. There were no more translation duties, but Julius was an invaluable help to me with practical things around the house. The following summer he went back to Vilnius to spend time with his family. I asked him if he could make the journey to Zagare and deliver the medication Isaac Mendelssohn had asked us to get for him. He agreed readily and on his return to Israel gave me a report on his visit to Zagare and news of Isaac and Aldona, all of which I forwarded to Joy.

Julius's studies were completed and his stay in Israel came to an end, though not without much deliberation and hesitation on his part. The deciding factor was Ieva and their decision to get married and build their lives in Vilnius. This was a wedding invitation I could not refuse. I set off for my second trip to Lithuania.

The wedding took place in the summer of 2004, and it turned out to be a three-part affair. First came the civil ceremony at the Vilnius municipal wedding palace. A number of other weddings were taking place that afternoon, and there was a big crowd in the outside courtyard, each wedding party waiting its turn. Some of the brides wore white lace gowns or satin crinolines; Ieva wore a simple flowered dress and looked beautiful. The ceremony, conducted by a young woman in a formal black-and-white outfit, was short and simple, with no religious content. An organ played background music followed by the "Wedding March"; there were photographs, handshakes, embraces, and a toast to the bride and groom.

Our party then drove out of town to a distant wooded hillside; cars were parked at the foot of the hill and we climbed up the steep path. At the summit was a flat grassy area, surrounded by trees, with a stone altar in the center. Here we were greeted by a group of pagans, one man and five women, who were preparing to conduct this second part of the wedding ceremony. In recent years Lithuania has witnessed a revival of paganism, a polytheistic or animist set of beliefs, based on nature. Ieva and Julius wanted to add some spiritual content to their marriage vows; as a Jewish or a Christian ceremony was neither appropriate nor available to them, they opted for a pagan ritual as a neutral alternative. The pagans, who were dressed in blue and white robes of homespun linen with white crocheted caps, lit a fire on the altar, scattered grain and salt, and offered sips of honey and mead to the guests. Slowly we circled the fire while the priest chanted prayers, accompanied by a zither-type instrument. Roza translated his words for me; he was singing songs of praise, not to the gods, but rather to the elements of nature, with a call for universal love, peace, harmony, tolerance and goodwill.

From there we drove to a party given by friends of the young couple. There were two other guests from Jerusalem, Guy and Sarit, student friends of Julius, and together we added a tiny token of Jewish tradition to the wedding. I produced a glass for Julius to stamp on and break, and Guy recited in Hebrew Psalm 137, "If I forget thee O Jerusalem." Everyone shouted *"mazal tov"* and the food and drink and speeches took over. I offered a few words in English, which were translated into Lithuanian, saying that Guy, Sarit and I were the only ones not rejoicing, as we in Israel would miss our dear friend Julius. But we accepted and approved his choice and wished him and Ieva much happiness and success in their new life together.

Before leaving Vilnius I connected with the Yiddish Summer

School, an event that takes place every year under the auspices of Vilnius University's Institute of Yiddish Studies. The program director, Mendy Cahan, an old friend from Jerusalem, invited me to join the students on one of the outings. This included a visit to the Jewish cemetery to pay our respects at the tomb of the Gaon of Vilna and a jolly outdoor *klezmer* concert by the lake near the town of Trakai. In the evening we assembled at the Jewish Community Center, some sixty or seventy students, young and old, fluent Yiddishists and total beginners, Jewish and non-Jewish. All had come to Vilnius to study the language and the history of the vanished Jewish communities of Lithuania. We were addressed by Shimon Alperovitz, president of the Jewish Community of Lithuania, and Ilya Lempert, professor of history, with Mendy in charge and translating for those of us whose Yiddish was below par.

On this visit to Lithuania, Zagare was not on my itinerary. Instead, I did a round of the Baltic capitals, taking the bus from Vilnius first to Riga, Latvia, and then to Tallinn, Estonia. Riga has the feel of a big European city, one that can stand comparison with Paris or Barcelona, with its broad boulevards, art nouveau Jugendstil architecture, opera house, cathedral, a picturesque walled old city and busy port area. It has a lively cultural scene, with concerts and exhibitions in abundance, and plenty of good shops, restaurants and hotels. All in all an attractive destination for Western tourists, of whom there were plenty in 2004.

Riga once had a thriving Jewish community, and it would have been the Big Apple for the *shtetl* dwellers of Kurland. Of Jewish Riga there was little to see. As in Vilnius, the Jewish community of Riga came to an end with the coming of the Nazis in June 1941. Thousands had already been deported to Siberia by the departing Soviets and thousands more were killed by the invading Germans. In October 1941 those who remained were herded into the ghetto, where they were confined until 1943, when the ghetto with all its inhabitants was liquidated. Looking to visit the only synagogue still remaining today, I found it locked, with guards and a police vehicle outside to prevent people entering. Nobody could explain why.

In the heart of Old Riga is the Museum of the Occupation of Latvia. A monolithic windowless black granite bunker of a building, squatting on its cement block foundation, it dominates the historic main square, in raw contrast to the surrounding historic buildings, which date back to the fourteenth century. Built in 1971 by the Soviets to celebrate the centenary of Lenin's birth, it initially served as the Museum of the Red Latvian Riflemen. With the departure of the Soviets it was reincarnated as a museum whose aim, according to the museum's pamphlet for visitors, is "to show what happened in Latvia from 1941 to 1991 under the two occupying regimes." It was highly recommended by my guide book, and I readied myself for the visit. The exhibits – explanatory panels, photographs and documents, together with artifacts illustrating the suffering of those years – were impressive, and indeed very moving.

It took some time before it dawned on me that the displays dealt exclusively with the Soviet occupation, the period 1945–1991. There must be another floor, I told myself, with exhibits documenting the period of the Holocaust, the German occupation. Eventually I found what I was looking for: a single glass-fronted cabinet containing photographs of Jews being deported, a map of the ghetto, and a yellow star. Trying to understand, I reasoned that forty-five years of the Soviet occupation of Latvia merited more space than the four years of the Nazi regime. Understandably it was the Soviet period that was remembered and execrated by the Baltic peoples, who had indeed endured terrible suffering. What was missing and what I needed from the Museum of the

Occupation of Latvia was some documentation, some recognition and acknowledgment of the even more terrible fate of the Jews of Latvia during the German occupation. The tiny display cabinet was not enough. It was a turning point in my perception of the Holocaust.

Some years later Rose Zwi had a similar experience in Vilnius and noted:

> On one of the boulevards of Vilnius stands the government-supported Museum of Genocide Victims, known as the Genocide Museum. But it is not the Jewish genocide they are concerned with. It deals only with Soviet crimes against Lithuanians, equating the Soviet oppression of the Lithuanian people with the Nazi-inspired genocide of the Jews, thus obfuscating the true significance of the Holocaust. The Double Genocide, they call it, and it has inspired a plethora of articles in the press, statements by politicians and "learned" theses in academe. The objective of this misnamed "Genocide Museum" seems to be to shift guilt and blame for the Holocaust, to rewrite history.[*]

It seemed that even half a century after the Holocaust, it was difficult if not impossible for the new generation of Lithuanians (and Latvians) to acknowledge and come to terms with the crimes of their parents and grandparents.

---

[*] Rose Zwi, "2012 Unveiling of the Plaque," JewishGen Zagare page, http://kehilalinks. jewishgen.org/zagare/Rose%20Zwi.pdf.

CHAPTER FIVE
FINDING RUTH

My visit to the Riga Museum of the Occupation of Latvia was a turning point in my understanding of the history of the Jewish people of Lithuania and Latvia. In the years that followed I became aware of the new distortions and obfuscations that had begun to proliferate in the Baltic states following independence. The term *double genocide* (or *parallel genocide*) that was bandied about equated the Final Solution – the extermination of the Jews as carried out by the Nazis and local collaborators – with the suffering and persecution of the Lithuanians by the Soviets, thus belittling the Jewish tragedy and diminishing and distorting the role of the Baltic peoples in the perpetration of the Holocaust.

With the collapse of the Soviet Union and independence for the former republics, many of the painful issues had resurfaced on the public agenda. Lithuanians now had to face the truths of the wartime years and the Holocaust – the German invasion, local collaborators, the massacres, the ghettos and the mass graves. Jews who wished to reconnect with the land of their forefathers had difficult decisions to make in facing the issues and in relating to the new generation of Lithuanians. The Lithuanians for their part had to learn how to relate to the Litvaks, the remnant of their country's Jewish population – the survivors, the descendants and the diaspora.

I had learned much in the fourteen years that had passed since Zagare's eight hundredth anniversary celebrations in 1998. Now here in front of me was another invitation to visit Zagare – again from Joy. The occasion, the brainchild of Joy, Cliff and Valdas, was the dedication of a plaque in the Zagare town square commemorating the annihilated Jewish population of the town. It had taken them nearly a year of hard work and planning to turn the vision into reality. Without hesitation I signed on and began to make plans for my second visit to the ancestral *shtetl*.

As the program took shape I joined the team and was asked to serve as master of ceremonies for the occasion. I drew up a tentative list of speakers, asking people to briefly outline what they would say. In addition to our declared aim of commemorating the vanished Jewish community of Zagare, our intent was to make the gathering a gesture of reconciliation and acceptance, a joint project and coming together of Lithuanians and Jews, but – as Valdas put it – without fudging the history. The words *local Lithuanian collaborators* were inscribed on the plaque in three languages – Yiddish, Lithuanian and English – and they would be enunciated loud and clear, amplified by the loudspeakers, across the Zagare town square where the massacre had taken place. But our intention was not to settle accounts with the local population or to seek revenge. Was it not appropriate that some message of hope, however slight, would also be conveyed?

The answer came in a letter from Valdas informing us that there was a family in Zagare that was being considered for a Righteous among the Nations award by Yad Vashem, the Holocaust Martyrs' and Heroes' Remembrance Authority in Jerusalem. Edvardas and Terese Levinskas and Terese's sister, Lilija Vilandaite, had protected and saved Batya Trusfus and Ruth Yoffe, a grandmother and her granddaughter, hiding them in their home during the German occupation of Zagare. When approved, the award would be bestowed posthumously, and the son of the family, Leonas Levinskas, would receive it on behalf of his parents and aunt. Moreover, it so happened that the family home where Leonas and his wife, Zofija, were now living, that very same house where Jews had been hidden, was next door to Valdas's mother's house, where we would be staying.

I had read of another case, that of Miriam Schneider, a young Jewish girl of Zagare who had been saved by local townsfolk. Those people had been honored by Yad Vashem several years before. This was a new case and I asked Valdas to provide more details. He contacted Yad Vashem and received a laconic reply: "The file on the Levinskas family has not yet been considered by the Commission for the designation of the Righteous. When it is ready it will be submitted for the Commission's consideration."

From the window of my Jerusalem home I could see across the valley to the Yad Vashem building on the horizon. I decided to bypass phones and e-mails and go there in person to make my inquiries. My contact in the Righteous Among the Nations Department was Katya Gusarov, and she received me politely if unenthusiastically. She gave me details of the case in question. In 1943 an elderly lady and her granddaughter managed to escape from the Siauliai ghetto. They were rescued and hidden by Lithuanians just before the Germans killed most of the ghetto inmates in a murderous *Aktion*. All this took place some seventy years ago. Why had the case not been concluded? What was holding it up? Katya explained that every case approved by Yad Vashem goes through a careful procedure of checks and counterchecks. In this case, there was no direct personal testimony from the individuals who were saved that could corroborate the story.

In 1991 the granddaughter, Ruth Yoffe, had immigrated to Israel. She came to Yad Vashem and deposited testimony about members of her family who had been killed by the Nazis. But she had not left an address where she could be contacted. Katya had tried to find her, but without success. I asked Katya how she went about looking for people. She was vague: "We ask around, look in the telephone directory..." was her reply.

Back home I wondered if I could do any better. How to start? My friend Ruth Bachi, who has written several biographies involving research into European history, put me on the right track. "Go into the Internet," she said, "and Google the name you're looking for – what else?" I was dubious. Ruth Yoffe is a common name – it would bring millions of links to the screen. "So try the grandmother," suggested my friend, and that is what I did. Batya Trusfus, I typed, and up she came on the screen, in the center of a vast family tree, drawn up by Allan Blacher of London, a member of the Trusfus clan and an addicted genealogist. Within minutes Allan and I were exchanging e-mails. He told me there were cousins of Ruth living in Israel and gave me their telephone numbers.

I pursued this line of inquiry, but the cousins were unable to help. They knew their cousin Ruth had come to Israel, had married (a second marriage) and become very devout and religiously observant. She had withdrawn from contact with her secular Israeli relatives, and they had lost touch with her. I seemed to have come to a dead end. I wrote to Allan sending him some information that I had gathered from the Jerusalem cousins, with additions and corrections for the family tree. "Thank you," he replied, "I'll check my notes and correct the mistakes." An hour later he was back. "I found in my notes an address for Ruth – in Jerusalem. It may be out of date. Good luck!"

I didn't waste a moment: I leaped into my car and within half an hour I was in the Katamon Gimmel quarter of Jerusalem, cruising along Rechov Bar Yochai, a shabby, rundown street with tenement blocks of small old-fashioned apartments built in the 1950s for new immigrants. Allan had given me two numbers, presumably one a house or block number, the other an apartment number. But the house numbers on Bar Yochai Street ended at 18, and both the numbers I had were much higher. I asked passersby, and was told the numbers had all been changed some years ago. For several hours I pestered older people, hoping someone might remember, but without success. Finally a young woman in a corner grocery store solved the riddle, and pointed out the block I was looking for.

There were no names on the letter boxes in the entrance, and no names on the doors. I climbed three flights and knocked on the entrance of apartment 24. The door opened. A little old lady in a neat housecoat, her hair tidied away in a snood, peered at me, mistrust written all over her face. "Ruth?" I queried. "Ruth Yoffe? Ruta?" "Yes," she replied, suspicion growing by the minute. "Daughter of Riva, granddaughter of Batya?" I continued. "Riva – yes, my mother," she said. "Who are you, what do you want?" As gently as I could I told her: "My name is Sara, I come from Yad Vashem, and I would like to ask you a few questions." Curiosity and hesitation battled across her features, with curiosity winning out. Finally she said, reluctantly: "Come in. But take off your shoes – I've just washed the floor," and handed me a pair of slippers.

So began my first meeting with Ruth Yoffe. We sat down at the kitchen table, and gradually her initial wariness melted. Soon she was answering my questions and volunteering information. I could see that my unannounced and unexpected arrival on her doorstep and my persistent questioning was an unsettling experience for her. She was digging up memories from the long-forgotten distant past, and she constantly shook her head in wonderment. "I haven't spoken about these things, I haven't even thought about them for nearly seventy years," she exclaimed. From the material received from Yad Vashem I already knew the basic outlines of the rescue of Grandmother Batya and her little granddaughter. Talking to Ruth I was able to fill in some of the gaps, gaining a firsthand impression as seen through the eyes of a six-year-old child of what Ruth and Batya had gone through in those terrible times, and learning something about the noble people who had helped them.

Following the German occupation of Lithuania in 1941 and the initial slaughter of more than a hundred thousand Jews, there was some respite in the wave of killings. The smaller ghettos and communities such as Zagare had been liquidated. The remaining Jews of Lithuania were used for slave labor and herded into three main ghettos – Vilnius/Vilna, Kaunas/Kovno and Siauliai/Shavel in the north. The Siauliai ghetto inhabitants survived because of the need for skilled workers in the Wehrmacht engineering corps, the Frankel tanneries and the former Bata shoe factories, which provided essential services and goods for the German war machine.

Grandmother Batya and Ruth lived in the Siauliai ghetto for two years, crammed into one small room with other members of their family, three women and four children. Ruth's mother, Riva Yoffe, a doctor, had been sent by the departing Soviets at the outbreak of war to work in a military hospital in Russia; her father had been drafted into the Red Army and was killed in battle in 1943. Their children, Ruth and her brother Misha, had been left in the care of their grandmother. Together with them in the ghetto were two of Ruth's aunts, Eta and Irle, and her cousin Riva. Ruth remembers that there was another girl, a teenager, who looked after the children during the day when the women were taken to work outside the ghetto after the morning roll call. In the evening the women would return with food hidden in their clothing. If caught they could be killed. Grandmother Batya did not go out to work. Her granddaughter remembers her lying down, ill in bed. There was a folding sofa bed in the room, where they hid the valuables that the family had managed to bring with them from their hometown of Pasvitin. This was the currency used to buy the food that Lithuanians from outside would smuggle into the ghetto. The folding sofa bed was closed during the day. Ruth has a memory of German policemen coming into the room with a dog, asking for a drink and sitting on the sofa, with the family treasures hidden inside.

In November 1943 came the *Kinderaktion*, the roundup that would liquidate all the children in the Siauliai ghetto. The inhabitants had some advance warning and tried desperately to save the young ones. Somehow Ruth's aunt made a connection with people outside the ghetto. Ruth remembers a Lithuanian woman who twice came to the house and talked for a long time with Aunt Eta. Eta gave her some of the family's possessions to take out of the ghetto, as they would have to leave without any baggage. When the woman left after the first visit she took Aunt Irle and Riva with her. They were never seen again. Ruth gave testimony to Yad Vashem that they were killed when attempting to escape from the ghetto. The fate of the teenager who had been looking after the children is unknown. Next day the police came and said that those who remained would be kept under surveillance to make sure they did not escape.

Ruth sketched for me a map of the ghetto as she remembered it, the parallel inner streets encircled by an outer street. One side of the street was closed off by a barbed-wire fence, and under the barbed wire was an opening, a dip or hollow dug out of the earth and covered with a board. Ruth doesn't know who excavated it. One night the four remaining family members crawled under the fence through the dip and escaped from the ghetto. They were not observed. Some distance from the ghetto the same Lithuanian woman met them, by arrangement. She took them in a horse-drawn cart to a house, where they were hidden in the attic. From there the refugees were taken to different homes and were moved on whenever there was a fear they might be discovered. Batya, Eta, Ruth and Misha were among the few who managed to escape from the Siauliai ghetto. "We were saved by God," Ruth sighs as she remembers those tense hours of fear and danger. "We children were constantly told to be quiet." Her eyes fill with tears, her voice cracks as the memories come flooding back.

By the time I had finished talking with her, Ruth's suspicions had vanished. The new life that she built for herself in Israel is now centered on religious observance and study. She showed me how prophesies of modern events can be found in the text of the Hebrew Bible, references to Hitler and the Holocaust or perhaps to the Twin Towers 9/11 disaster, the words to be picked out by reading the letters across the page in a vertical or diagonal direction. She asked me whether I observed the *mitzvot* (religious commandments) and lamented my secular way of life. Nevertheless, despite the unbridgeable differences in our outlooks and lifestyles, we were able to communicate. When I left she hugged me warmly, and I promised to return. Further, she gave me permission to give her address and telephone number to Yad Vashem.

I hurried down the stairs and back in my car I immediately dialed Yad Vashem on my mobile phone. "Katya!" I exclaimed, "I found her! Ruth Yoffe – you've been looking for her for six years, since the file was opened in 2006. She is right here, just down the road, here in Jerusalem. You can contact her and get all the information you need." Katya was astounded, and said she would take me on as a detective for Yad Vashem's research department. I told her that Ruth had little recollection of her stay of two or three days in Zagare with the Levinskas family, but remembered clearly the Alekna family, who had looked after her for nearly a year. She had visited them in Lithuania some years ago and had a great affection for them. Katya said that minimal corroboration testimony from Ruth, details of dates and places, even if indirect, and of herself and her family, would suffice. She was confident that the award would now be made. In the following weeks Katya herself went to Ruth's home, interviewed her and made copies of family documents and photographs in her possession.

I was beginning to put together a picture of the heroism of the rescuers, and in particular of the Levinskas family of Zagare, whose son, Leonas, I was hoping to meet very shortly. In the Yad Vashem archives I found more material. The 1941 rescue of Ruth Yoffe and Batya Trusfus was organized by a group of Lithuanians led by Juozas Petrulis, a resident of Siauliai. Other members of the group were the Kalendra and Alekna families, and – from Zagare – Edvardas and Terese Levinskas together with Lilija Vilandaite, sister of Terese. They were longtime friends, and members of a circle of Tolstoyans, individuals who followed the ideas and lifestyle of Lev (Leo) Tolstoy – a melding of spirituality and manual labor. After the war Eta Trusfus wrote an account of their noble actions and sent it to the Lithuanian Communist Party, asking for them to be officially recognized:

Dear Friends!
Forgive me for taking up your precious time. This letter is written in gratitude and wonderment for the people who sacrificed themselves in order to save other people. I am one of the few Lithuanian Jews who were saved from the Fascist criminals. All my family – father, two sisters, family of my brother, husband and all his family – were murdered by the Hitlerites. Those who were saved – myself, my mother and the two small children of my sister – were saved only because of the self-sacrifice and the

humanity of some Lithuanian citizens. In my opinion, their acts were acts of heroism. I would wish that all our country would know about them, the finest sons and daughters of our country.

Juozas Petrulis now lives in Vilnius and works at the National Education Museum. Even though I did not know him before, we – myself, my mother and my niece and nephew – lived in his apartment in Siauliai until other hiding places were found for us. Notwithstanding the danger to his life, he did his duty as a human being. Afterwards, when my mother [Batya Trusfus] an old lady of eighty, had to leave the previous hiding place and return to Siauliai, Comrade Petrulis came in the full light of day to the place where she was waiting for him, and found another hiding place for her. My sister's daughter [Ruth Yoffe] stayed with him in Siauliai until rumors began to circulate that Petrulis was helping Jews and was a Communist. Petrulis was forced to leave Siauliai, but before leaving he found another hiding place for the child with good-hearted people.

Andrejus Kalendra, a resident of the village Senukai, hid me, my nephew [my sister's son, Misha Yoffe] and another Jewish child. For eleven months he fed us and protected us from danger. Povilas and Paulina Alekna from Lepine protected my sister's daughter [Ruth Yoffe] for eight months, fed her and looked after her as if she were their own child. The Levinskas family, and their sister Lilija Vilandaite, residents of Zagare, for eleven months hid, fed and looked after my mother [Batya Trusfus].

All these people, who did so much for us, were not known to us before. As time passes and we are more distant from the terrible period and the terrible happenings, the feeling of wonderment at their doings grows ever stronger, as does our wish to show our gratitude. I would like everyone to know about them, not only their acts of heroism, but also their acts of love for the homeland.

SIGNED: *Eta Trusfus Kolodnaya*, now living in Kazan [Russia]*

---

* Collection of the Righteous Among the Nations Department (Yad Vashem Archives M.31.2/12424).

Juozas Petrulis, an archaeologist and a scholar of Lithuanian folklore, arranged for Batya Trusfus, Ruth Yoffe and other members of the family to come to his home, where they were first hidden after escaping from the ghetto. When the neighbors' suspicions were aroused he arranged new hiding places for them. In 1967 Ruth visited Petrulis, and she remembers him with great affection and gratitude. After the war Ruth's mother Riva Trusfus Yoffe wrote to Petrulis:

> There are no words to express my thanks to you for saving my family. I cannot thank you enough for what you have done, and I will express my profound gratitude till my dying days. My daughter Ruta calls you "the good uncle" and my mother Batya calls you "the angel."*

Petrulis's friend Edvardas Levinskas in whose house Batya and Ruth were hidden wrote an account of the episode:

> In the last days of the occupation, we hid a Jewish old woman, who had escaped from the Siauliai ghetto. Nobody turned us in, even though the neighbors had their suspicions. We were very happy that in the autumn of 1944 her son came from Moscow and took her. He wanted to give us money, but we told him we did this out of charity and not to make money. Both of them thanked us, and we parted as friends. The old lady was the widow of the pharmacist, Yitzhak Trusfus.**

Edvardas Levinskas's son Leonas was twelve years old at the time. Many years later he wrote down his memories of the months when Grandmother Batya was hidden in his home:

---

* Cited in Sofija Binkiene, ed., *Soldiers without Arms* (Vilnius: Mintis, 1967), 265.

** Edvardas Levinskas's original Lithuanian testimony from the Collection of the Righteous Among the Nations Department (Yad Vashem Archives M.31.2/12424), translated into Russian, then into Hebrew, then into English.

In 1944 an old lady came to our house, with a little girl. I was told that they were Russian refugees. Later the little girl was taken to another family, and the old lady stayed with us. At this time we lived in a very small house, with a kitchen and two small rooms. The old lady was always kept out of sight in one of the rooms. At this time a German unit was based in Zagare. Because Mother and her sister spoke German, the Germans used to drop in to our house for a chat and to listen to our radio. On the door between the rooms there was no lower strip. The old lady, who didn't hear well, wanted to listen to the conversation, and came right up to the door, and her shoes could be seen on the other side of the door. It was lucky that no one asked who was in the other room. Because the Germans used to come to our house, it helped us to hide her. No one would suspect that a Jew was hiding in the house where Germans came to visit. The old lady had a typical Jewish appearance, and had a Jewish accent. She knitted for us socks and gloves, which we wore and were grateful for. The little girl was called Ruta Yoffeite, and the old lady was her grandmother.[*]

I heard the final chapters of the Trusfus-Yoffe saga from Ruth on my next visit to Rechov Bar Yochai. After the end of World War II the surviving members of the family – Batya, Ruth, Misha and Eta – left Lithuania, never to return. They moved to the Russian city of Kazan, where Ruth was reunited with her mother. Here she spent the remaining years of her childhood, trained as an engineer, married, and gave birth to her son, Ya'akov. Following the breakup of her marriage she became increasingly attracted to Jewish spirituality and learning. Throughout the Soviet era religious observance and practice were prohibited, and Ruth was frustrated in her attempts to learn Hebrew and study Jewish subjects. Emigration to Israel was not allowed in this the period of the refuseniks. With the collapse of the Soviet Union and the

---

[*] Collection of the Righteous Among the Nations Department (Yad Vashem Archives M.31.2/12424).

opening of the gates Ruth did not hesitate. Soon she was on her way to Israel, to fulfill her heart's desire and make a new life in Israel for herself and her son.

When Ruth came to Yad Vashem to fill out the form detailing the life and death of six of her relatives, she was not aware of the Yad Vashem project that honors the Righteous among the Nations and commemorates their heroism in saving Jewish lives. Thus she did not provide the testimony needed to make the prestigious award to the people in Lithuania who had rescued her and her grandmother. It was this missing testimony that was holding up the award to the Levinskas family of Zagare.

The Yad Vashem guidelines for approving an award are very strict. Only persons who actually risked their own lives and the lives of their families in order to protect the life of a Jew qualify. For the most part the populations in Nazi-occupied countries turned their backs and did nothing as their Jewish neighbors were sent to concentration camps and systematically murdered. Pleas for help by Jews fell on deaf ears. There were those who took advantage of the situation to seize and occupy Jewish property and steal the belongings left behind. There were those who actively collaborated with the Nazis and themselves carried out unspeakable acts of violence and terror. The moral and physical courage of the few who stood out against the Nazi horror, often paying a great price, is inestimable. Help extended to Jews by their rescuers could take many forms: hiding them in their homes, providing them with false documents in order to disguise their Jewish background, smuggling and assisting people on the run to escape from areas under Nazi control, rescuing children by taking them to convents and orphanages or even raising them as members of their own families. In order to properly document and recognize their bravery and sacrifice, Yad Vashem established its Righteous Among the Nations Department.

The aim of the department is to substantiate and honor the heroism of these noble individuals and to show them and their descendants that their courageous actions are remembered and appreciated by the Jewish people as a whole. To date, more than seven decades after the Nazi terror, some 24,500 persons from forty-four countries worldwide have been awarded the medals and certificates of the Righteous among the Nations. For each one a tree is planted in the gardens surrounding the Yad Vashem campus, and all the names are inscribed on the Wall of Honor. Every honoree receives a certificate and a medal inscribed with his or her name and the Hebrew saying "He who saves a single life saves an entire universe" (Talmud, *Sanhedrin* 37a).

The award ceremony usually takes place in the individual's home country, with the presentation made by the Israeli ambassador to that nation. Having set in motion the procedure for completing the recognition of the Levinskas family as Righteous among the Nations, I was hoping that the committee would now accelerate their deliberations. If the Levinskas award ceremony could be combined with our memorial dedication it would greatly enhance both events and add much to the significance and solemnity of the occasion.

CHAPTER SIX
THE PLAQUE

The Yad Vashem proceedings to recognize the Levinskas family as Righteous among the Nations had been set in motion and the wheels were turning – but slowly. There was no word from Katya and it seemed unlikely that the committee's deliberations would be completed in time for the award ceremony to be part of our memorial dedication. The date had been set for July 13, 2012, and we were pleased to learn that the town's festival organizers had incorporated the event as part of the annual Zagare Cherry Festival. We were on the map. Preparations moved into high gear and arrangements were beginning to fall into place.

As the date neared, the ad hoc committee was convening daily by e-mail and conference call: Joy in England, Cliff in the United States and Valdas in Lithuania, together with Rose Zwi in Australia, filmmaker Rod Freedman also from Australia, Julius in Lithuania and myself in Israel, with occasional input from Yiddish scholar Dovid Katz, always on the move.

Valdas was our man on the spot and it was he who handled all the logistics of the event. With invaluable support from the regional chief architect, Daiva Bickiene, permission had been obtained to place the plaque in the town square, opposite the cultural center. Much significance was attached to this decision taken by the Zagare municipal authorities. Dovid Katz described the event on his website (www.defendinghistory.com):

> ...a local Lithuanian businessman, members of the municipality, and foreigners of Litvak origin team up to produce Lithuania's *first and only (?) town center plaque* that tells the simple truth about the fate of the town's Jewish population....* [The plaque] is placed right in the center of town, rather than at a mass grave site deep in the forest; that might well be a first in modern Lithuanian history.**

Valdas wrote to Rose Zwi, reminding her of their earlier exchange of letters and inviting her to take part in the dedication ceremony:

> **Valdas to Rose:** Joy, Alex and dozens of members of Lithuania Link have invested huge amounts of time, finance and patience into Zagare's community over the last 20 years. If not for them, we would have not known our own history, we would have not traveled the world and seen ourselves from outside, and obviously not have known you and your book. We wanted to ask if there was any chance inviting you to Zagare to participate in the opening of the square and the memorial plaque this summer. Myself traveling often to Singapore for business I know what kind of trip it is.... If not possible, I promise to keep you informed and send pictures of the memorial once installed.

> **Rose to Valdas:** I was so pleased to receive an email from you after all these years. I remember how heartened I felt when I

---

* Dovid Katz, "2013 on Wrong Note in Capitals of Poland, Ukraine, Lithuania," Defending History, http://defendinghistory.com/londonfogpart2/44532.

** Dovid Katz, "Trilingual Memorial Plaque Unveiled on Zhager Town Square," Defending History, July 13, 2012, http://defendinghistory.com/tag/lithuanian-shtetl.

received your letter. At last, I thought, someone of the younger generation is brave enough to accept the reality of what happened in 1941. Whenever I felt despairing about the continued denial of those terrible times, I read those lines of yours "*... Last Walk in Naryshkin Park* has moved and appalled me more than I can say.... I want to say to you how full of pain and sorrow I am on behalf of my community.... I am continually aware of the tragedy. There ARE people who remember and care about what happened...." I still have your letter which makes me feel that my cry into the wilderness, the pain of writing that book, was not in vain.

I was pleased to hear that you, Joy and Cliff have worked on placing a memorial plaque in the town square. Is the square where the marketplace used to be? What will be the wording of the plaque, and in what language(s) will it be? It remains a place of great sorrow for me; I couldn't bear walking on it when I was in Zagare. But perhaps there will be reconciliation at last and real regret for the past, for those terrible times.

Thank you for inviting me to come in July when the plaque will hopefully be in place. I am very conflicted about coming, even to such a positive event. There is still much I have to work through in my mind and heart. And, of course, I am no longer young and the journey from Australia is arduous. But there is much I still have to come to terms with, and if I can manage to do that, I shall come. I'll let you know within the next week or two whether I will undertake it. I know I can rely on you to keep me informed if I decide not to come.

I was very sad to hear about the death of Isaac Mendelssohn, as I refer to him. He was an inspiration to me. And his wife, Aldona, was a wonderful woman who was a very good influence on him, and a most hospitable person. I remember them fondly. I never met their sons. Thank you for that wonderful photograph of him, standing in front of the sign Zagare, as though to say, this place is my home, no matter what anyone says. Valdas, thank you for writing to me.

Valdas also wrote to filmmaker Rod Freedman after viewing his film *Uncle Chatzkel*, a documentary of the life of Rod's great uncle

Chatzkel Lemchen, a distinguished lexicographer and scholar, who had grown up in Zagare:

Valdas to Rod: First of all thank you very much for the *Uncle Chatzkel*. Amazing story and very nice film you have created. I lived in Vilnius (Zverynas) a 5 minute walk from your uncle not knowing what a great man lives just round the corner... I'm 35 this year. I was born and grew up there (in Zagare) by the Naryshkin Park. Only after Lithuania got its independence back people started to talk a bit about the Jewish tragedy. First of all there were graves, where one day the plaques changed from "Soviet citizens" into "Jewish victims." Then as I grew bigger I started hearing the stories, studied more history, got in touch with Joy Hall (Lithuania Link) and read *Last Walk in Naryshkin Park*. From then I started to understand what history holds in our small town. I have a grandmother who is 84 this summer and she remembers a lot from her childhood. When I asked her she started to talk about the Jewish tragedy, about the Lithuanian collaborators and the killings. She was also friends with Isaac and my uncle went to school with his sons. They live in Vilnius now. I keep on researching.

I cried with you watching the film; my heart bleeds whenever I think of what happened with the Jewish community and of what my grandma told. Therefore I need all info about the past. Like your uncle – it's fragile and it's disappearing; you have to catch every word and every story you can grasp. I am ready to listen and record and pass it over to others. The Jewish spirit is alive and I and my family want to make it stronger, if there is a way, to do something to ease the pain.

Therefore from now, even though I know Zagare will remain the sad recollection for Jews, may I once again call it your home. Sad, still bleeding, but the roots – like you said – are such and they are priceless.

You and family are welcome back to visit, stay, remember. We are slowly building new Zagare and you can again be part of it in all possible ways. Like Mrs. Rose Zwi said, "may there be more walks in the Naryshkin Park."

We all felt it was important that there be a strong representation of Jews of Zagarean descent at the event. I wrote to people I thought might be interested and passed on the invitation to various media outlets. My first success was in persuading Rose to come. She had already turned down Valdas's invitation, but my promising to look after her and to share the room Valdas had booked for me changed her mind. I invited Roger Cohen, columnist for the *New York Times* and *International Herald Tribune*, who was of Zagarean descent. A few months previously, following the death of Isaac Mendelssohn, he had written a fine article entitled "The Last Jew in Zagare."* I also contacted Rod Freedman. At one time we had corresponded about having his film screened on Israel TV and now I renewed the connection. I discovered that he was currently based in Spain and in touch with Valdas. It was not difficult to persuade him to join us, and he proved to be a great asset to the gathering.

The Zagarean diaspora was assembling. In the months leading up to our event Cliff found himself traveling in South America, and at one point told us he would have to cancel the trip to Zagare. But he reconsidered his priorities, and like the rest of us was on a plane heading for Lithuania in time for July 13. Cliff is the founder and editor of the Zagare website www.kehilalinks. jewishgen.org/zagare, and he had alerted the entire mailing list with an invitation. Three members of the Woolfson family from England – Raymond, Gill and Hazel – picked up the message and joined our party. Altogether there were eight of us of Zagarean descent – from Australia, South Africa, the United States, Britain and Israel – accompanied by a few friends and spouses.

A notice in the *Jerusalem Post* attracted some attention, and I was contacted by a number of Israelis of Zagarean descent. In the event none of them was able to come but we remained in

---

* *New York Times*, November 7, 2011.

touch. Israel's embassy in Riga serves both Latvia and Lithuania. I sent an invitation to the ambassador, inviting her to speak at the ceremony as our guest of honor. After some exchange of e-mails we were delighted to receive word from Riga that the ambassador or her deputy would join us on the day and would speak on behalf of Israel.

Much thought had been given to the wording of the inscription. Once it had been decided to have a trilingual plaque in Lithuanian, Yiddish and English, Cliff worked on a draft of the English text, which was then translated into the other two languages. Dovid Katz took responsibility for the Yiddish and Valdas for the Lithuanian translation:

> For hundreds of years Žagarė (in Yiddish – Zhager) had been home to a vibrant Jewish community. Zhager had many Jewish shops and was a center of commerce for merchants from here and a range of other towns. Many of their shops surrounded this square. Zhager was also famous for its many Hebrew scholars, the "Learned of Zhager." German military occupiers and some Lithuanian collaborators brought the region's Jewish men, women, and children to this square on October 2, 1941. Shooting and killing of the whole Jewish community of Zhager began here and continued in the forests nearby. About 3,000 Jewish citizens were killed.

It was decided that at the dedication ceremony Rod would read the plaque text in English and Valdas would read the Lithuanian version. Dovid Katz agreed to read it in Yiddish and was also given the honor of leading the assembly in reciting the Kaddish.

Valdas was working around the clock. He made decisions regarding the Lithuanian speakers, Jewish and non-Jewish. He finalized accommodation and travel arrangements for the overseas visitors. He coordinated our event with the municipality and with the Cherry Festival organizers, and he set up media coverage. In the week preceding the ceremony he spent hours checking the engraving of the inscriptions on the plaques and ensuring they would be mounted on the plinth in good order. He sent us photos of the town square, where reconstruction work was in progress with paving being laid right up to the last moment. And he was there a day before the event to greet us as we arrived – the Zagareans of the diaspora coming home.

I had arrived in Vilnius four days earlier, met at the airport by Julius and his mother Roza. Julius and Ieva had invited me to stay with them, in the house they had built for themselves on the outskirts of the city. In Soviet times people were given plots of land for growing vegetables and raising poultry to supplement their food rations. Under the new regime permits to build had been issued, and Julius and Ieva had taken advantage of the revised regulations to construct for their family a fine wooden house with a large garden. Here I was looked after, cosseted and spoilt. I was happy to do some sightseeing in the Old Town with Roza, go for walks in the forest, spend time with Julius and get to know his family. My time with Rose Zwi was the icing on the cake. We had so much to talk about and I was very pleased to find her in good health and – no less important – in good spirits. She had come to Vilnius the week before to be with her family. She introduced me to her cousin Freda, daughter of her Uncle Leib about whom she has written so movingly in her book.

In the evening Rose and I were guests for dinner at Julius's parents. Roza and Rose hit it off straightaway, conversing in Yiddish. Here too it seemed like family. It dawned on me that unknowingly I had joined the club and become a Litvak, like Roza and Rose – though a somewhat inadequate Litvak in that I have no knowledge of Yiddish. I had always thought of myself as Jewish and English. My Israeli identity came later, confirmed by my

Israeli passport, my Israeli family, my Hebrew-speaking children and grandchildren, and the home my late husband and I had built for ourselves in the Jerusalem hills. Now my involvement with Zagare added a new dimension.

The next morning Rose, Julius and I set off for Zagare. Before leaving Vilnius we stopped at the local supermarket to buy provisions for the Friday night celebration planned for the next evening. We found good quality Israeli wine, several loaves of braided *challah* (Sabbath bread), sprinkled with poppy seeds, and a packet of candles. We drove north in Julius's car through the fields and forests of the flat countryside, a pleasant and uneventful journey, reaching Joniskis in good time. There we met Cliff, who had gone to look at the restoration work being done on the town's two abandoned synagogues, the White Synagogue and the Red Synagogue, both of which had fallen into disrepair. Joniskis has no Jewish community, but Cliff through his voluntary work with Lithuania Link had set in motion the project for restoring these two handsome buildings.

From Joniskis it was a short drive to Zagare and the grand meeting in Sarah Mitrike's garden of the descendants, the Lithuania Link activists, the accompanying relatives and friends, and the local people. It felt like a family reunion, even though most of us had never met before. Sarah Mitrike, née Rabagliati, was now back living in Zagare with her husband and young daughter. The Zagare Cherry Festival, which Sarah had founded, was in its eighth year, and the summer festivities were due to start the next day. Nevertheless, Sarah and her husband, Saulias, made time to welcome the visitors from overseas with a barbecue picnic in their garden. The afternoon sunshine alternated with intermittent rain showers, sending us running into the house, as Saulias kept an eye on the grilling meat sizzling on the charcoal.

We stayed at the Mitrike house talking comfortably as the day drew to a close, waiting for Valdas to return from Riga after picking up Rod Freedman at the airport. We then set off to our lodgings, some in private homes and some in the town's recently opened modest B & B. Four of us were billeted in the newly renovated home of Valdas's mother, who had generously vacated the entire house for the duration of our stay. Rose and I were allocated one room and Joy and her friend June were in the second bedroom. We found the kitchen fully equipped and the refrigerator and cupboards full of provisions. Valdas's mother dropped by to welcome us and to deliver a dish of cottage cheese dumplings and a bowl of cherries for our supper. We spent the rest of the evening going over our speeches and the running order for the next day's dedication ceremony. The afternoon rain had washed the air fresh and clean. Our beds were comfortable and it was time to turn in and get some sleep.

The group of descendants had begun to coalesce into a family unit: Cliff Marks from America; Rod Freedman and Rose Zwi from Australia, both with roots in South Africa; my cousin Joy and Roger Cohen from Britain; cousins Raymond and Hazel Woolfson also from Britain; and myself, Anglo-Israeli. Joy's friend and Lithuania Link activist June Hall and Raymond's wife, Gill, rounded out the party. Our Zagare adventure had begun.

Next morning Valdas took Rose, Rod and me to meet our next-door neighbors, Leonas and Zofija Levinskas. It had rained during the night; there were puddles on the unpaved road, and after splashing from our house through the Levinskas garden our shoes were muddy. Zofija opened the door to us and said something to Valdas. He explained: "She says to take off your shoes – she has just washed the floor," the very same words with which Ruth Yoffe had greeted me when I knocked on her door in Jerusalem six weeks before. The streets of Jerusalem are not as muddy as those of Zagare, but the habit had remained with Ruth after all the years.

An elderly couple in their eighties, Leonas and Zofija Levinskas received us warmly. Zofija hugged Valdas, who as a child had been in her kindergarten class. With much pride, Leonas showed us the album of press cuttings, certificates, photographs and other documents collected over the years. The parents of both Leonas and Zofija had risked their lives and the lives of their families to save Jews from the Nazi terror. I had earlier received from Yad Vashem translations of the accounts of those terrible times that Leonas (born 1931) and his father Edvardas Levinskas (1893–1975) had written, in Lithuanian. These were deposited with the Jewish Museum in Vilnius, who had forwarded a copy to Yad Vashem. Here is the English version of testimony by Edvardas Levinskas:

> In the summer of 1940 when the Soviet government took over in Lithuania, I was appointed supervisor of primary schools in the region and the town of Panevezys.* I worked there until the beginning of 1941. Afterwards I began to work in adult education in Panevezys and this was more difficult, mainly because my views and my philosophy of life did not fit my job. I could not cope with this and so I resigned my post. We moved to Zagare and here together with my wife's sister Lilija we started to work in agriculture – growing fruit and flowers. My wife and her sister had learned this work from their parents. Lilija had done this work all her life. Then World War II came to Lithuania and to Zagare. The town was occupied by the cruel Nazis. During the occupation I did not have any official job and I had nothing to do with the Nationalists.** Their private life, their false ideas were foreign to me. In the spring, summer and autumn I had a lot of work in the fields. In my free time, mainly in the winter I busied myself with translating the writings of Tolstoy into Lithuanian.
>
> In these terrible times we suffered many tragedies. In Zagare

---

* Also known as Ponevezh, the original home of the Ponevezh Yeshiva.
** Lithuanian extreme right-wing parties.

the Jews were severely persecuted; the children, pregnant women, the sick and the disabled were mistreated and abused, and also the strong and healthy population. Women were raped and then murdered. On October 2, 1941, the date when the Jews were rounded up and murdered, my wife was with them, and she was grabbed because she tried to protect the Jews. At night some of the Lithuanians who called themselves White Band activists started to kill the rich Jews and to take their possessions. It became clear that soon the rest of the Jews would be killed. My wife traveled to Siauliai to speak to the commissar regional governor about the situation of the Jews. She thought that everything was the initiative of the Lithuanian activists. She was not allowed to speak to the commissar. She went to other people whom she knew, wrote a letter, and sent it by post to the commissar, in her name and in the name of other righteous people. She asked them not to debase the German people by killing innocent Jews, and instead to display humanity. She signed this letter with her own name and address, and added that she was herself of German origin.

When the commissar received the letter he decided that she must be insane, and gave orders for her to be killed together with the Jews. To carry out the order he sent an SS officer on the day of the mass killing of the Jews to tell the murderers to bring my wife to the police station. The killers came to our home and took her away. By chance she managed to escape death because of the intervention of Burgermeister Mayor Rakshchu. He found out that my wife was at the police station, went there, persuaded the German SS officer to meet him, and managed to make him drunk. Afterwards, he put the officer in his car and ordered the driver to take the officer to Siauliai. Later, towards evening, the mayor came to the police and released my wife and let her go home. But this was not the end of the story. Two weeks later, the same SS officer came and took out all my family from our house. He demanded that my wife recant all the main points in her letter to the commissar, and if she wouldn't agree he threatened to shoot her. He was very angry, but he didn't dare use force and simply commanded my wife to keep quiet about the fate of the Jews of Zagare.

We sat and talked with Leonas and Zofija in the very same room where Batya Trusfus had been hidden by Edvardas and his wife, Terese, for nearly a year. Ruth had stayed there only two or three days and had no recollection of the Levinskas family. But Leonas remembered the little girl, then six years old. I told him how only a few weeks ago I had found her, now aged seventy-five, in Jerusalem. He was very excited and asked me to send him a photograph of her. In his written account he retold his still vivid memories of the German occupation of Zagare and the massacre of the Jews in October 1941:

> My parents and all my family knew many of the Jews of the community. I studied at school with Jewish children, and we were friends. When I was ill, as a child, the Jewish doctor looked after me. My aunt Lilija Vilandaite, my mother's sister (1900–1948), lived with my family. In 1941 when the Germans conquered Lithuania and put the Jews in the ghetto, she managed to obtain from the authorities permission to use Jews as laborers in our fields. Through them we maintained connection with the ghetto and helped the people with food. The workers came to us and returned, without armed guards. Some of the ghetto guards allowed people to bring food inside. Sometimes I went with Aunt Lilija to bribe the guards, and afterwards we took food into the ghetto and visited our friends. The Zagare ghetto was surrounded with barbed wire, and was guarded by armed guards, mainly White Band activists. In the Zagare ghetto were Jews from Joniskis and from other places. When we discovered that in Naryshkin Park they were digging a deep pit it was obvious to everyone that now they were going to kill the Jews. We advised our laborers to run away and hide with people. But they wouldn't believe us; others did not want to leave their relatives, and returned to the ghetto, and so they were killed with everyone. It is our belief that on that day more than three thousand victims were killed. I do not know if anyone was saved. No one spoke about this, and I was a child at the time. A special unit of German soldiers supervised the killing.

The officers took photographs and even filmed the happening. Another special unit came, killers who were in action throughout Lithuania. Among them were men born in Zagare and nearby villages. After the war most of them were sent to prison in Soviet camps and died there. There were some who became crazy from feelings of guilt, or became alcoholics.

This is how the killing was organized: they ordered all the Jews on the day of the massacre to come to the Zagare town square and bring with them documents, food and clothes. They were told they would be taken to work camps. When everyone came to the square, surrounded by the killers, the German officer gave a speech, telling them that they were being taken to a place where there were would be no problems, no suffering. People began to panic, and the murderers began to shoot with explosive bullets and most of the people were lying on the ground, completely blown apart. The wounded were killed off immediately. Afterwards the bodies were loaded on trucks and taken to the Naryshkin Park and thrown into the pit. The rest of the ghetto inhabitants were taken from their houses by the murderers, who ordered them to lie down on the trucks, one on top of the other. Those that were alive were beaten and raped. By the pit they were ordered to undress, take off their shoes and jump into the pit. The first layer of bodies was covered with earth, and then another group of victims was shot and thrown into the pit. All the killers were drunk. Some of them couldn't cope with the situation and started to run away, and they were shot. On the day of the murders, I saw in our street some men running away from the town center. The shots went right by me. I fell down on the ground and crawled to the garden of our house. I saw that these men entered the courtyard of another house. I heard people shouting and the noise of trucks.

Next day I went to school, as usual through the town square. The dead bodies had gone, but there were pools of blood, lots of documents, scraps of food, pieces of torn clothing and remains of flesh and blood. Even though the square was flushed down with water from hosepipes by the fire brigade, the blood stains remained for another month on the paving stones. I saw how they brought to the pit more Jews, who had escaped the first killing, mostly women and children and one old man. There were people who went to the ghetto and took everything from the houses. Gold, silver, jewelry and money, and all the valuable things were taken by the murderers. The less valuable things were sold at a public auction. My family was very upset by the happenings. My father's hair went white because of this. And in protest I refused to learn German in school (and I never regretted this).

A month later my father and I returned from the fields which were just outside the town. A German officer caught up with us, with skull and crossbones badge on his cap. He took out his pistol with one hand, and with the other hand he grabbed my father by his beard, and said to him: "You are a Jew." He kicked me aside with his boot. Father said that he was Lithuanian, married to a German, and if the officer would come with us, his wife would explain everything to him, in German. The officer ordered my father to walk in front of him, with his arms raised, and walked behind him with the pistol aimed at my father. Mother explained that my father was not a Jew, despite his beard. The officer asked her why her family had not returned to Germany. Because of this the family was suspect, and would suffer the same fate as the Jews. Afterwards he gave me a piece of chocolate, which I threw into the toilet after he left.

In Leonas's album was a newspaper cutting of an article about the Tolstoyans of Lithuania, with a photograph dated 1933 of a group that included their leader, Juozis Petrulis, alongside Edvardas Levinskas. In 1980 Petrulis was recognized by Yad Vashem as Righteous among the Nations, and the Kalendra and Alekna families were honored, posthumously, in 2008. Now Leonas was awaiting recognition for the heroism of his parents and aunt. With the addition of the important newly recorded testimony given by Ruth the file would shortly receive final confirmation. In Jerusalem Katya Gusarov had assured me that the award would be approved, but she said it might take time to complete the arrangements. We had hoped to combine the Yad Vashem award ceremony with the memorial plaque dedication but it was not to be. Final confirmation and the award ceremony came only the following year. With Valdas translating, I explained all this to Leonas, who was, understandably, somewhat disappointed. I told him that we, the Zagarean descendants, were this day honoring him and his family on behalf of Ruth and her grandmother, and I presented him with a gift from Jerusalem.

From the Levinskas house our group of eight descendants went to Naryshkin Park to visit the mass grave and lay flowers, each of us with our own thoughts about family, fate and "what if…"

Rod Freedman was thinking about his great grandparents, as he wrote:

> On Friday morning, we went to the Jewish Genocide (translation from Lithuanian signpost) site in Naryshkin Park. It's a ten-minute walk from the town square. This is where the main massacre took place and where my great grandparents are buried. It remains a chilling and beautiful place. A U-shape of dense, flowering shrubs marks the pits and mass graves. The surrounding tall trees filter light onto the memorial plinth, inscribed in Lithuanian and Yiddish. Fifteen years ago when I was filming, I dug up an oak seedling from the adjoining forest and planted it in the clearing with the help of Isaac and his wife, Aldona. I placed stones around it, hoping it wouldn't be mown down. I dubbed it "The Lemchen Tree" in memory of our family and asked Isaac and Aldona to look out for it. They've both since died, so imagine my surprise to find that it has survived. It will be there for a long time.

For Rose Zwi, whose grandparents, aunts and cousins are buried there, it was a place where, as she wrote later in her account of our visit:

Unbidden images rise of the massacre of 1941. It began here and ended in the woods surrounding Naryshkin Park, where the dead and injured were buried in prepared pits. The grave, it is said, heaved for days. These images must now be put aside. We are here to mourn our dead and seek reconciliation with a new generation of Zagareans whose acceptance of the truth of the massacre is symbolised by the unveiling of the plaque....

From Naryshkin Park we went back to the town square, where the workmen were still feverishly paving the area around the plaque. We were relieved to find it in place with the three inscriptions engraved on the metal plates and mounted on the plinth in good order. We all adjourned to the local café opposite the site for *borscht* and *blintzes* and a quiet moment of fellowship before the ceremony ahead of us and the arrival of the guests, participants and audience.

Showers and sunshine were the backdrop to the memorial gathering, and umbrellas were much in evidence. The paving stones had been laid and the plinth with the three plaques was in place, covered with a cloth. Two microphones with loudspeakers had been set up, one for the speakers and one for the translator. There were rows of plastic chairs, and people were beginning to gather in the town square, the audience numbering about 150 people. The Israeli ambassador had sent her apologies, and in her place came the deputy head of mission, Liat Wexelman. She arrived from Riga bearing a large bouquet of flowers. "Who should receive these?" she asked me. I replied that no individuals were being honored at the ceremony – but that perhaps she should lay them at the foot of the plinth after she spoke.

Valdas translated throughout, into English or Lithuanian as required. The proceedings were opened by the head of the local council. I then introduced the guest of honor from the embassy and added a few words:

We are gathered here this afternoon for the unveiling of a memorial plaque. It is a joint effort, the initiative of friends and supporters in the local community, together with Jews of Zagarean descent from overseas. The event itself and the setting in the town square of Zagare are of great significance and are profoundly symbolic. This plaque is dedicated to the Jewish community of Zagare and to the memory of those who were killed on October 2, 1941, in this place, murdered by the Nazis and by their Lithuanian collaborators. World War II was a terrible period for the Jewish people, and for the peoples of the Baltic republics. Our gathering here today is an attempt to come to terms with the past, to acknowledge what happened, to nurture the spirit of reconciliation, to continue to build trust, to accept and to remember. This is our goal.

Joy's speech was in the same vein. She spoke about Lithuania Link, about building bridges, and about her deep connection to and affection for Zagare and its people. Cliff talked about the significance of the occasion for the group of descendants who had gathered in Zagare from overseas. Then Valdas described how he had been affected by learning of the town's history and about the motivation for erecting the plaque in the center of the town. He hoped it represented a new beginning. Vidmantas Mendelsonas spoke movingly about Isaac Mendelssohn, his late father, and promised to uphold his legacy. The heroism of Lithuanians who had risked their lives to save Jewish families was recalled in the story of Miriam Schneider, who had been rescued by people in Zagare. Her son Edmundas Tiesnesis spoke about those who had been honored by Israel as Righteous among the Nations. Special mention was made of the Levinskas family and the award soon to be made by Yad Vashem. Letters of greeting from Lithuania's minister of foreign affairs, Audronius Azubalis, and Member of Parliament Petras Austrevicius were read out to the assembly.

The speeches were all appropriate, and all were sincere. But the importance of the occasion lay in its context – a context of cooperation between Jews and Lithuanians, of coming to terms with the past, an open acceptance and acknowledgment by Lithuanians – or at least some Lithuanians – of the terrible history of collaboration with the Nazis, a context of reconciliation and of looking ahead towards a better future. So much of what we accomplished was due to Valdas, the prime local mover and shaker, and to Joy's initiative in setting up the Lithuania Link connection between the locals, the descendants, and others from overseas. The event was sponsored by local funding, which covered the costs of the plaque and the dedication ceremony. We, the Jews from outside, were not allowed to contribute. But we were permitted a free hand in the program and the choice of speakers, and we tried to find a golden path between the harsh notes of history and the sweet sounds of reconciliation.

Of our little band, Rose Zwi was closest to the legacy of the past, and it was she who unveiled the plaque. She spoke with much emotion:

> As I stand before this plaque, I am overwhelmed by the thought that my parents and I might have lain in the mass grave together with my father's family had they not left Zagare in the 1920s. I never knew my father's family, but I mourn them to this day. "Remember us!" their unquiet spirits seem to call from the grave. As though one could ever forget. They do not ask for vengeance, only remembrance. They will always be remembered. And, in the language we would have had in common, I say: *Mir zeinen doh!* We are here.

Valdas had tied down the cover to prevent it blowing off and Rose unveiled the plaque with some difficulty. It started to rain again as Rod, Valdas and Dovid read aloud the texts in English,

Lithuanian and Yiddish. The downpour continued, then cleared, leaving glittering tears on the metal plates. At that moment bells tolled from an unseen church. As people gathered around the plaque, Dovid Katz began to *daven*, rocking and swaying, intoning the ancient Aramaic words of the Jewish prayer for the dead in the very place where our forebears had been corralled for the massacre. With the final *amen* of the Kaddish prayer, the memorial dedication ceremony came to an end.

We had overrun our allotted time, mainly because of the time needed for translation, and all of us cut our speeches drastically. But our audience stayed with us, attentive to the end, rain showers notwithstanding. It was hard to believe that the months of planning and preparation had brought us to this moment of completion. But there was more to come. In the town's cultural center, in the town square right opposite our plaque, another Jewish-related event was in progress, also part of the Cherry Festival. A talk, in Lithuanian, about Jewish history was followed by a concert of Jewish music – a singer of Yiddish songs and three *klezmer* performers. The audience loved it and roared with applause.

When it turned out that the event was to take place on a Friday, the suggestion was made that our dedication ceremony should be followed by a Kabbalat Shabbat, a festive Sabbath eve gathering. This needed organizing, and in the absence of any hotels or eating places in Zagare, the task fell to Valdas, with Julius lending a hand. They found a charming chalet outside the town and provisioned a buffet supper of salads, cheeses and smoked meats – and bowls of cherries. The wine and *challah* from Vilnius were added to the feast. Some thirty people came to our gathering – local friends and supporters from Zagare, members of the Jewish communities of Siauliai, Vilnius and Riga, and our band of descendants from overseas. There was a feeling that something important had been accomplished and there was much conviviality and talk and laughter. Rose, Hazel and I lit the Sabbath candles we had brought and recited the traditional blessings over the candles, the wine and the bread.

Rod Freedman, who was one of several speakers at our informal gathering, later recalled the words that he had spoken that evening:

> I told why I'd first come to Lithuania and Zagare and talked about Uncle Chatzkel, and Avraham and Rachel, my great-grandparents. I recalled how we, our family, had thought of Lithuania as being in the past and impossible to visit until my cousins Emile and Ondine Sherman came to see Uncle Chatzkel and opened the door. I'd been filled with anxiety and tension when I first arrived in Zagare to film in 1997. I'd been immersed in the events of 1941 to the point where I couldn't really see or feel the present. Zagare (and Lithuania) in my mind was a dark, repressive, threatening place. I now felt very differently, thanks to the actions of Valdas and his supporters in this project. It has made a big difference realising that there had been people who'd helped the Jews. History has been recognised and the truth has been told, even to the extent that the local collaborators are mentioned on the plaque. It's only one of over 200 towns in Lithuania where massacres occurred but it is significant.
>
> Back in 2000 I did an investigative program called *One Last Chance* that dealt in part with the issue of the lack of honesty in Lithuanian memorials. Under the Soviets, plaques stated only that "Soviet citizens" had been killed by the Nazis. Then later, they noted that Jews had been killed by the Germans, but rarely had it been conceded that Lithuanian collaborators had participated. This is part of the significance of this event along with the fact that until now, almost all memorial plaques have been discreetly hidden outside the dozens of towns in the forests where the killings usually took place. I ended by saying that I now feel connected to Zagare and welcomed. It's been a great journey of reconciliation.

The dark presence of Zagare and the dozens of other towns like it with their massacre sites have stayed with me in the fifteen years since I went to Lithuania to make the *Uncle Chatzkel* documentary. The contrast between the present beauty and the past horror is too much to integrate. This journey has helped me at least feel that there is acknowledgement of those past horrors and not to feel a stranger in the home of my ancestors. I am grateful to all those involved in organizing the event, especially Valdas Balciunas, for reaching out to the Jewish descendants of Zagare in a spirit of warmth, openness and honesty.

Undoubtedly our ancestors were with us in spirit and were joining in our celebration. When had Zagare last had a Kabbalat Shabbat, heard a concert of *klezmer* music, or joined in the reciting of the Kaddish prayer? When was the last time Jews had gathered together in the central square – the marketplace where our forefathers had once lived and worked, traders in timber, flax and grain, brewers of vodka and schnapps, innkeepers, teachers, barbers, seamstresses and shopkeepers, who struggled to make a living for their families? As Rose Zwi had declared earlier that day, "We are here!" The sun was setting over the fields as we returned to Zagare, flooding the sky with rose, violet and turquoise. There was a feeling of peace and tranquility in the air as darkness fell.

Next morning Rose and I went back to Naryshkin Park, heading for the Cherry Festival. The field was filled with stalls selling cherry-themed knickknacks and all kinds of local food fried, grilled or roasted on the spot. There were weight-lifting competitions and pony rides for the children, and all the fun of the fair. I found a gift to bring back to Jerusalem for Ruth Yoffe – a small box inscribed Ruta, the name she had been called as a child growing up in Kurland. A Baltic senior football match was advertised, with one of the teams listed as Makabi of Vilnius. The game started late so we never got to see the Jewish footballers of

Lithuania, but Rose fell into conversation – a Yiddish conversation – with Yossi from Siauliai, the father of one of the team members.

From there some of us went to the Jewish cemetery, remembered from my previous visit. The site was still neglected but the grass had been cut and an attempt had been made to restore the headstones. On the way back to the town center we met and spoke to a family who had been visiting the nearby church. They showed much interest in our visit to Zagare and welcomed us warmly. All the members of our group made similar comments on the friendly feelings in the town. This was in marked contrast to the experiences and impressions of Rod and Rose on their earlier visits, when they had encountered nothing but suspicion and hostility.

Our last visit before our party broke up was to the House of Pots and Pans. The exterior of the building, walls to rooftop, was covered with pots and pans and pan lids, glittering in the sunshine. It was the workshop and garage premises of an eccentric local sculptor, Edmundas Vaiciulis, an avid collector of junk and castoffs. The building had in former times housed the cloth-dying workshop run by Rod's family. In the garage were some huge containers that could have been the dye vats. The sculptor's daughter took us to the courtyard, where her father's collection of *objets trouvés* was on display. Piles of household and industrial objects were stacked there in random heaps, unlabeled, in total disorder, the discarded leftovers of homes and workshops long vanished. The girl noted that we were interested in the Jewish history of Zagare and said she had some things to show us. She disappeared indoors and returned carrying a Torah scroll. It was a sad sight. The parchment was dirty and badly torn at the edges, and the whole scroll was roughly bundled up like a roll of old newspapers. The girl laid it on the dirty floor for us to get a better look and started to unroll it. Horrified to see the precious manuscript treated so carelessly, we picked it up and spread it open on a nearby table. It appeared to be not very old, with fine calligraphy, but in poor condition. Apparently it had been found inside the wall of an old house, behind the plaster work, presumably hidden there by a Jewish family fleeing the town. The girl also showed us a jar with old coins, seemingly Russian or Polish, but we found no Jewish connection in them.

And then at the back of the courtyard I came across the musical instruments – three trumpets, a euphonium, two saxophones and a bugle – decayed, rusty, broken, covered in dust and cobwebs. I called to Rose. These must have belonged to the band of her Uncle Leib, her father's younger brother. It had to be. We touched them, picked them up, and looked at them for a long time. Rose was weeping. In her book she had written about Leib, recounting the stories and memories told by her Aunt Leah, his widow, and others who remembered the charismatic trumpeter and leader of the Zagare band:

> Impressed by his musicality, the choirmaster taught Leib the rudiments of music.... Leib saved every hard-earned kopeck to buy a trumpet.... At sixteen [he] joined the band of the local fire brigade.... He was young and handsome, and loved music and dancing. The young women in the *shtetl* fell in love with him, and he with them.... What everyone is agreed on…is his passion for music. He played on every possible occasion, in any milieu.... [H]e formed a band, and played with non-partisan enthusiasm at socialist, religious and even Zionist functions.... "Leib Yoffe the musician?" people still say. "I remember him well. When Leib stood up to play solo, everybody stopped dancing or romancing, and listened."*

---

*   Rose Zwi, *Last Walk in Naryshkin Park* (North Melbourne, Victoria: Spinifex Press, 1997), 20–26.

Following the German invasion of Lithuania, Leib managed to escape to Russia with Leah, his young wife, already pregnant. Like Isaac Mendelssohn and many other Lithuanian Jews he joined the Sixteenth Lithuanian Brigade of the Red Army. One of Rose's informants told her that Leib had been a member of the brigade orchestra. He died in battle in 1943. Freda never knew her father. Leah and Freda survived the war years in Russia living on a *kolkhoz*, and returned to Vilnius after the war. Now Rose was holding in her hand a trumpet from the Zagare band, one that in all probability Leib had once held to his lips. It was the closest any of us came to our ancestors, a poignant moment for us all.

CHAPTER SEVEN
ACCEPTING

T he events of our three days in Zagare are whirling in my
mind, demanding resolution. The gathering turned out to
be a bringing together of people and ideas in a way that none
of us had anticipated. Back home in Israel, I am surrounded
by press cuttings, diary, photos, and a laptop overflowing with
e-mail correspondence, out of which I must structure a coherent
narrative. And for this I need to examine carefully the issues
involved in "accepting."

In the months leading up to the Zagare dedication event and in
the months that followed, I had become increasingly aware of the
growing mistrust and tension between the Litvaks – the overseas
diaspora plus the tiny community of Jews living in Lithuania
today – and the Lithuanian establishment. It had surfaced in our
correspondence regarding the wording of the plaque – a brief
discussion about the exact number of victims. It wasn't even
an issue; it was simply Valdas's determination "not to fudge the
history" and to get every detail right. The number inscribed on
the obelisk at the mass grave was three thousand. In order to
get confirmation of this Valdas had turned to the Genocide and

Resistance Research Centre of Lithuania. The director of the research department referred him to a document dated 1941, drawn up by the German Einsatzkommando, listing the number of men, women and children killed in the Zagare *Aktion*, a total of 2,236. Rose picked up on this exchange and wanted to know more. She herself had done much research on the October 2 massacre for her book:

Rose to Sara: Who is this Director? What is this institute? A Lithuanian apologist for the Holocaust? Is this another denial strategy?

Sara to Rose: I hear your voice, loud and clear, and your concern. I have no answers to your questions, which you are certainly entitled to ask.... The issue is the precise number of the murdered, and Valdas is waiting to receive confirmation from the so-called Lithuanian Genocide and Resistance Research Centre – whatever that may be. Rose – I don't want you to get involved in this – it would be too painful. But there are questions unanswered and I will ask them on your behalf. OK? .... No, you are not paranoid. There has been denial and falsification of history and we should be on our guard – but without being obsessive or paranoid. I shall ask the questions that need to be asked. But I am determined to enjoy myself in Zagare, and I will make sure you enjoy yourself too.

Rose to Sara: My dear, dear Sara – thanks for your understanding and support. I too want to go to Zagare and enjoy being with friends, and finally meet wonderful people like Valdas, who is so dedicated to reconciliation.... I'll behave and not disgrace you – if I need to, I'll mourn privately.

Sara to Rose: Me again – you've really got me going on this! I followed up Valdas's contact, whom he consulted re names and numbers; he is Arunas Bubnys, Director of Research at the Genocide and Resistance Research Center of Lithuania....

From their website I got the impression that the GRRCL is something of an establishment outfit, focusing primarily on atrocities committed during the Soviet regime, with very little to say about those of the German occupation. Hardly a mention of the Holocaust or the Jews, and no mention of Lithuanian collaborators.... I then checked on Bubnys...here I got a more positive impression. His book *The Holocaust in Lithuania between 1941 and 1944* does not fudge the issue, and pretty much tells the story as it is. Low-key, not blazing with anger and outrage, qualifying some of the verdicts with a balanced comment – which is how history should be written. Right? To me he sounds credible. He concludes with the sentence "Although the Final Solution was organized and initiated by the Nazis, it would not have been carried out so quickly and on such a scale without the active support of part of the Lithuanian administration and the local population."* That is a key remark, and not easy for a Lithuanian government employee to enunciate. So I think he is OK. I then wrote to Dovid Katz and asked for his take on the GRRCL. He directed me to his Defending History website and the entry in the tongue-in-cheek Dictionary of Lithuanian-Jewish relations reads: "Genocide Center = obfuspeak for a center interested in all except the one genocide that occurred in the country where it is located." ...So we'll have to take it or leave it. I'm going to leave it, and be content with giving Bubnys a clean bill of health.... Rose my dear – your instinct was right, spot on. And this bit of research has opened our eyes and put us on our guard. But we move on. And our revenge is that we're here, we're there, we're back in Zagare, and we're going to have a great time together. Right?

About this time the newspapers were full of reports on the Juozas Ambrazevicius-Brazaitis reburial scandal. The puppet prime minister, a collaborator who headed Lithuania's provisional government during the early months of the Nazi occupation in

---

* Arunas Bubnys and D. Kuodyte, *The Holocaust in Lithuania between 1941 and 1944* (Vilnius: Genocide and Resistance Research Center of Lithuania, 2005), 51.

1941, had lived and died in exile in the United States during the Soviet period. His remains were being brought back to Lithuania for a major state reburial ceremony with speeches and military honors, in the presence of leading establishment figures. One of those scheduled to speak at the ceremony at Kaunas University was historian Arunas Bubnys – to whom I'd given a clean bill of health. I went back to the Defending History website and found a quotation from an interview with Bubnys where he claimed there was "'no evidence' Lithuanian anti-Soviet activists were engaged in mass murder."

In her book *Once Were Slaves*, Rose Zwi tells the story of her husband's family, Lithuanian Jews who eluded the Nazi genocide and survived the terrible hardships of Soviet exile:

> The Perlovs were victims of the two largest totalitarian states that had risen from the ashes of World War I: Nazi Germany and Soviet Russia. Both imprisoned "enemies of the state" in concentration camps, where they were overworked, starved and stripped of human dignity. Though similar in many ways, there was a *fundamental difference* [emphasis added] between them. The primary objective of the Soviet prison camps was economic. Although millions died from starvation, disease and exhaustion, there were no extermination camps in the Gulag. The Soviet state needed their labour to fulfil its unrealistic economic goals…and exploit the vast under-populated areas in the far east and far north of Russia.… Nazi concentration camps had an entirely different agenda: the genocide of the Jews of Europe.*

In this "fundamental difference" lies the answer to the monstrous Double Genocide theory now being spread abroad, which equates the suffering of Lithuanians under the Soviet regime with the

---

* Rose Zwi, *Once Were Slaves: A Journey through the Circles of Hell* (Darlinghurst, New South Wales: Sydney Jewish Museum, 2010), iii.

Holocaust inflicted by the Nazis upon the Jews. In Lithuania's case the Double Genocide theory serves to dwarf and conceal the role played by Lithuanian partisans who collaborated with the Nazis in the annihilation of their Jewish fellow citizens.

> **Sara to Rose:** I have been thinking and thinking again about the legacy of Lithuanian collaborators and how we Jews, both in Lithuania and outside, should relate to it today, seventy years on. The fact that the atrocities were so horrific and so widespread is one thing; attempts at reconciliation such as our event, such as Joy's Lithuania Link, such as the various showcase institutions in Vilnius that you mention are another. But the problematic one is the ambiguity and hypocrisy of the authorities in the two decades since Lithuanian independence, and their failure to acknowledge and come to terms with the past as the Germans have done. This was evidenced in the recent return and reburial with honor of Brazaitis, prime minister in the puppet regime of 1941, and many other incidents diligently documented by Dovid on his website – incidents which give clear support to the Double Genocide theory, to anti-Communism, and to renewed anti-Semitism. Have you read Ellen Cassedy's *We Are Here: Memories of the Lithuanian Holocaust*? She writes about her visit to Lithuania where she searched for roots and took a hard look at relations between Lithuanians and Jews. She asks: "Could I honor my [Litvak] heritage without perpetuating the fears and hatreds of those who came before?"* Like us she tried to build bridges and to find Lithuanians who are ready to engage in dialogue and to acknowledge the past.

There are those who disagree with our conciliatory stance – in particular, Holocaust survivors, those whose family members suffered and those who speak for them. I have to say that I understand their skepticism; in most cases I even agree with their

---

* Ellen Cassedy, *We Are Here: Memories of the Lithuanian Holocaust* (Lincoln: University of Nebraska Press, 2012), 10.

reservations. In the words of Dovid Katz, questions need to be asked, and this he does diligently and relentlessly on his Defending History website. I have had several exchanges with Dovid on the issue.

> **Dovid to Sara:** Real conciliation is proceeding with real Lithuanian people, not the government hacks who so successfully manipulated [...people...] into actual falsifications of history.... It's about moral backbone and honesty.

Perhaps the key lies in Dovid's phrase "real Lithuanian people," focusing on them as the people with whom we should be engaged in dialogue. Without question the "government hacks" and "silver-tongued elites" should be challenged. Falsification, misrepresentation, distortion, obfuscation and hypocrisy must be fully exposed, countered and condemned without reservation or qualification. But presenting a different point of view or offering a new interpretation of the facts does not amount to falsification, nor does it weaken the basic argument. There was so much suffering in the "bloodlands" during those terrible years; no single community has a monopoly – not as victims, not as perpetrators. Understanding and listening to the other side of an issue does not amount to an endorsement or acceptance of the opponent's argument.

When looking at the fallen tombstones in the Jewish cemetery in Zagare and afterwards in our exchange of letters, Cliff and I had talked about the issue and found that we were in agreement. Yes, we said, in any discussion there is always another side that needs to be addressed. Yes, even in Holocaust matters.

> **Cliff to Sara:** My main thought is that it is rare when people really put themselves in others' shoes – really understand where they are coming from and try to see the other side of an issue. I

think the Jewish community may not recognize, at times, how much non-Jewish Lithuanians (note that people are still referred to as either Lithuanians or Jews and the idea that Jews could be considered "Lithuanian" seems to be absent) really felt oppressed by Russia/Soviet Union. While Jews react negatively (rightly so) to the Double Genocide idea, and to the Genocide Museum in Vilnius (because it denigrates the suffering of the Jews and what was done to them), that does not mean that there was not real suffering under the hands of the Soviets. Maybe it is hard for some Jews to see the genuine feeling of Lithuanian patriotism on the part of Lithuanian partisans during the war. The difficult part is that they often were also anti-Semites that killed Jews.

I could never understand how some Lithuanians greeted the Germans with open arms when they marched in. But after understanding the history of Lithuania being under Russian control for centuries, then getting their independence after WW I, then having the Russians come back in 1940, I could see a little of how they might want the Germans to kick the Russians out. Of course, I never could understand killing one's old neighbors, especially women and children – that still is beyond my understanding. But I think we Jews have to understand a bit more how negatively the Soviet Union was viewed by non-Jewish Lithuanians. Maybe Stalin was not Hitler but he was pretty bad.

Cliff and I attempted to grapple with the issue; should we (like Joy) reach out to Lithuanians, accept and welcome official attempts to mollify and appease and make up to the Jews and accept these gestures at their face value? Should we (like Valdas) put aside the bitterness of the past, talk to the new generation and get on with the future? Or should we (like Ephraim Zuroff and Dovid Katz and many of the survivors) look history in the face, study and document it, make sure it is not forgotten, and pursue justice and retribution? Cliff and I, both of us inveterate fence-sitters, decided that if Lithuanian officialdom did or said nice things (such as agreeing to the Zagare plaque, and taking part in our dedication ceremony with official letters of support sent by government ministers), we would accept these gestures and appreciate them at face value, lip service and window dressing notwithstanding, whatever the motive, whatever the underlying hypocrisy.

In my file was a translation of the letter sent to us by Audronius Azubalis, Lithuania's foreign minister, and read out at our dedication ceremony. He said all the right things:

> The Holocaust map of Lithuania is dotted with black spots, terrible places where Jews were massacred.... We cannot delete them from our historical memory...we must condemn those who in collaboration with the Nazi occupiers failed the test of humanity...we must look at our past openly and honestly.... I bow my head in memory of those killed, I bow my head to the rescuers of Jews, heroes of Lithuania.

Yet this was the same official who not long ago quipped, "It is not possible to find any difference between Hitler and Stalin except in the size of their moustaches: Hitler's was smaller." Dovid has no patience for such double-talk; we however accepted Azubalis's letter. But we made sure that those words "local Lithuanian collaborators" were heard by everyone in the Zagare town square.

Then came an unexpected development. A few months later I was approached by members of a Zagare family, who asked – hesitantly – if I could do some research for them in Jerusalem. They wanted to know if there was truth in the stories they had heard that one of their ancestors had been among the collaborators who had joined with the Nazis in murdering the Jews of their town. I replied that I was willing to make inquiries and look up records in the Yad Vashem Archives. It was a rare instance of readiness to face up to and accept the past and to speak about the unspeakable, an indication perhaps that attitudes in Zagare were beginning to change.

Lithuania is not alone in its failure to confront and deal with the legacy of the Nazi occupation. After the collapse of the Soviet Union, latent anti-Semitism resurfaced in many countries of Eastern Europe, manifested in attacks on Jewish institutions, tombstone desecrations and unrestrained racist hooliganism at sporting events. At government levels there has been a reluctance to bring Nazi collaborators and war criminals to trial. The academic world often acquiesces in a distorted account of the Nazi era. The one-sided museums, the Museum of Genocide Victims in Vilnius and the Museum of the Occupation of Latvia in Riga, are further signs of this ambivalence. Some seven decades have passed since the defeat of Nazi Germany, but the issues of local collaboration with the enemy and the betrayal of the Jewish communities have yet to be resolved.

Germany, today reunited, has over the past half century made serious efforts to face the past, to educate the young generation and to compensate the victims. A start was made in the 1950s with reparation for Holocaust survivors introduced by Chancellor Konrad Adenauer. These payments were defined as a partial recompense by the West German government for the "unspeakable criminal acts...perpetrated against the Jewish people during the National-Socialist [Nazi] regime of terror."*

For decades France struggled to resolve the legacy of the Vichy collaboration regime. The ready acceptance of Nazi racist ideology by the Vichy politicians and the role of the French police in the roundup and deportation of French Jewry are still passionately debated. French writers and filmmakers have kept the issues before the public, and a number of war criminals and collaborators have been brought to trial. Eastern Europe has lagged behind. Lithuania

---

* Reparations Agreement between Israel and West Germany, signed at Luxembourg, September 10, 1952.

and the other former Soviet republics have yet to find their way to a resolution, on an official level, of the legacy of the Nazi era.

Only the passing of time will bring the events of the past into true perspective, when victims and perpetrators will have passed from this world. As historian Bernard Wasserstein notes:

> More than any other religion or people, Judaism and Jews are centrally concerned with collective historical memory. The desire to stare history unflinchingly in the face is in tune with Jewish tradition, and arises, in its current form as applied to the Jewish catastrophe in Nazi Europe, from the most well-meaning of motives. Within limits the exercise is socially necessary and healthy. The problem is to define those limits.*

In Israel, to this day, the terrible history of the Inquisition and the expulsion of the Jews from Spain more than five hundred years ago is very much remembered and remains part of the national consciousness. Together with our resilience, we Jews have long memories.

From here we move on. Enough of the cons – it was time to look at the pros. For me there was above all a profound feeling of satisfaction that what Joy and Valdas had envisioned had been realized, and that together we had accomplished what they had set out to do. The story of the vanished community – the fate of the victims and the role of the perpetrators – was now engraved on three metal plates set in the town square where the massacre took place, for all to read. In the welter of signposts, plaques and memorials scattered throughout Lithuania, commemorating more than two hundred murdered Jewish communities, the Zagare plaque is the only one that is centrally positioned in the very heart of town or village, clearly visible to all those who pass by.

---

* Wasserstein, *Vanishing Diaspora*, 130.

Following the breakup of the Soviet bloc, in the period when Lithuania's application to join the European Union was being considered, attempts had been made at the highest level to prove that the country was genuinely looking to resolve the terrible legacy of its collaboration with the Nazis in the annihilation of its Jewish population. The rash of plaques that appeared on the walls of buildings in Vilnius and Kaunas was part of this strategy, together with support for Jewish institutions and events and the welcome given to Jewish visitors in search of their roots. But as Dovid Katz noted on his website, the signposts and plaques in the smaller towns and *shtetlach* were placed near the mass graves in the forests outside the town or village, barely noticeable to visitors and local residents. Dovid wrote:

> The reconciliation inherent in the historic truth being told in three languages in a plaque in the center of [Zagare], in a project conceived and brought to fruition by Lithuanian-Jewish partnership, and without the presence of national politicians, can become a template for emulation across the land.*

As Dovid pointed out, no less significant than the location was the Lithuanian-Jewish partnership that gave birth to the memorial. The genuine gesture of friendship and goodwill extended to the people of Zagare by Lithuania Link was the starting point for the project. Dreamed up by Joy, and supported by Alex, Sarah, Cliff and the other Friends of Zagare, Lithuania Link is proof that it is possible to move on, to find new paths and new ways of thinking about the past and relating to it.

I went back to Alex's insightful words: "[Following independence much of Lithuania's] inconvenient history has been side-

---

* Katz, "Trilingual Memorial Plaque Unveiled," http://defendinghistory.com/tag/lithuanian-shtetl.

stepped or rubbed out." Working with the people of Zagare, Alex came across instances – words and deeds – of racism, intolerance and discrimination directed against gypsies, immigrants, women and Jews. He wrote that it was never the aim of Lithuania Link to change attitudes and opinions, but the interaction with the local population did encourage awareness and a more international and accepting attitude towards the other. Alex continued: "There is a lot to be said for raising awareness as a corner stone for change. At the same time there is a fine line between raising awareness and forcing people to come to terms with their own history." He concluded that involving people in projects with a common purpose allows them the space to learn, accept and move forward from what has happened in the past.

Unexpectedly, Lithuania Link, led by Joy and Alex, had gone far beyond Joy's original plan of sending care packages, and had made a significant contribution towards healing the wounds of the past. Through their Lithuania Link projects Cliff and Sarah also helped to raise awareness of the Jewish heritage of the district: Cliff through his involvement with restoring the Joniskis synagogues and Sarah through the project for documenting the tombstones in Zagare's two Jewish cemeteries.

The other side of the Lithuanian-Jewish partnership was the indispensable dynamic engendered by Valdas. Starting with his translation of Joy's speech at the eight hundredth anniversary celebration in 1998, bringing her words to the people of Zagare (and to the president of Lithuania), and reinforced by his reading of Rose Zwi's book, Valdas went on to study the fate of the Jewish community of his town. Over the years his dedication to reconciliation and acceptance found expression through the projects of Lithuania Link in Zagare. The scholarship he was awarded by Lithuania Link enabled him to travel abroad, his first encounter with the West. In Britain he spent time on a dairy farm, where he studied feed-milling technologies, and on his return he went on to develop Golden Grass, a horse feed business in Lithuania. Today he is a successful entrepreneur, married, and father of a young daughter.

Valdas to Sara: I keep asking myself what life in Zagare would be like now if the Holocaust did not happen. What Lithuania would be like if the Holocaust did not happen. Before the plaque production I searched for historical facts, local people's opinions, all the information available about the Holocaust in Zagare. There was very little to find. Fifty years of Soviet rule have erased the Jewish heritage except the buildings and the cemeteries from Zagare's face. Pretty much from people's minds too. There was no reason for people to talk about it: some locals participated in the massacre; some took the belongings; some lived in the Jewish houses after the community was eliminated. Naturally there is little will to come to terms and it is easier not to think about it for many locals whose parents lived together with the Jewish community. The fact that Jews were rich, a rather closed circle, a different religious community, and most Lithuanians were poor, did not lead to very close relations either. I spoke to many people but most I heard was from my grandma and the Levinskas family.

You see, Soviet era – how I hate to say it – made my parents' generation indifferent about people around them, not willing to analyze, and of course not to take any responsibility. I do not blame them for this. All of them had gone through their own Soviet tragedy. But that does not solve anything to do with Jews either. The massacre picture is there. There is no way of escaping it.

With the new relations with the Jewish descendants we hope to build more justice, acknowledging the fact of collaboration with the German army, the value and volume of the lost Jewish community and its input into the history of our hometown. We believe there is a lot to be rediscovered identifying those people, families, lives and more through the descendants of families who managed to leave Zagare before the Holocaust.…

Since Lithuania got its independence back the situation

towards the Holocaust has been steadily improving. There is more and more acknowledgment every day. The government slowly is announcing the names of German collaborators; we get more information about Litvaks, their lifestyle and their input into prewar Lithuanian culture. Never mind few nationalistic radical outbursts; today's Lithuania is considered a safe place to live for the small remaining Jewish community and an increasing number of visitors from abroad. I put big hopes towards the new generation. Therefore as most of Zagare's community is lost in their outlook I will speak out on behalf of all the community.

Valdas's determination to face the truth and his dedication to teaching the history of those terrible years to the younger generation of his community culminated in the erection and dedication of the plaque in the heart of Zagare.

Valdas to Rod: My initiative to unveil the plaque is a small step forward to explain to the locals the truth. I do not want my children to grow up in a world of lies. I do not want the future of the town to be built on a distorted foundation. A dozen of locals were collaborators, a few names I know. Many people had work in Jewish craft shops; many Lithuanians lived or still live in Jewish houses. All Lithuanian community in one way or the other benefitted over taking the property. That is probably why people did not want to hear the story and that is why I'm even more willing to tell it. The Soviet generation I do not have any hopes for. My target is my generation and the younger. The more I talk the more response and understanding I get from others and I slowly achieve small results.

Isaac Mendelssohn's death the previous year had left Zagare with a zero Jewish presence. The link with the Zagarean diaspora was central to Valdas's vision of the future. Rose's decision to make the journey from Australia and be with us on the plaque dedication day was of great significance for everyone.

Valdas to Rose: A lot has changed in Lithuania and Zagare during the last 20 years. The nation is slowly healing from Soviet depression – freedom, democracy and improving economy let us evaluate the past more soberly compared to those days you saw Zagare last time. However, the Soviet generation (my parents' generation) born from 1930 to 1975 remains psychologically damaged, unable to value the past clearly. The Soviet regime left scars in Lithuanian minds erasing values of democracy, human personality, private property, etc. These people who are still mayors, party leaders, civil servants and others are still in power and the healing is not as fast as I wish it was.... But never mind this, the Holocaust is recognized and acknowledged and commemorated every year. The Holocaust is *nationally* acknowledged as the biggest wound in Lithuania's history.

Valdas's unfailing energy, his good spirits, warmth, empathy and optimism endeared him to us. The three days in Zagare were sufficient for a close bond to be forged between him and the little band of eight descendants. Though we were meeting for the first time, our gathering together in Zagare was a kind of "homecoming" and we straightaway coalesced and formed a "family" unit. Clearly our grandparents would have known each other, and there was a reaching out and sharing of the legacy of our ancestors which continued to resonate after we dispersed. For a brief few hours there was once again a Jewish presence in the town. Rose spoke for us all when she declared, "We are here." For Rod and Rose, whose immediate family members were buried in the mass grave, the return to Zagare was a *yahrzeit* (a memorial anniversary), a lighting of *nerot zikaron* (memorial candles), a closure, putting to rest the unquiet spirits of the past.

RIGHTEOUS AMONG THE NATIONS

T he final scene was acted out eight months later on March 19, 2013, in the depths of the Baltic winter. It had taken the best part of a year for Yad Vashem to complete its deliberations and grant the title of Righteous among the Nations to the Levinskas family. Some months after my return from the Zagare dedication ceremony, Katya informed me that the committee had finally given its approval and that the medal and certificate were on their way to the Israel embassy in Riga via diplomatic pouch. The ambassador would conduct the ceremony and make the award. The date was set, and everyone was delighted to learn that the event would take place in Zagare. This would save Leonas and Zofija a journey on icy roads to Vilnius or Riga and enable family, friends and townsfolk from Zagare to be present. The embassy asked me to put them in touch with local people who could help with making the arrangements. Valdas was only too ready to serve as the local representative, and Julius was on hand as the Israeli-Lithuanian go-between.

The embassy asked us for suggestions regarding a venue. Joy, Cliff and I immediately thought of the cultural center in the town square, facing the memorial plaque. But Valdas had another idea. "Culture house will be no problem," he wrote, "but how about the school? How about teaching the new generation? Why not in front of 300 children so they start to know what it is all about?" He approached the school principal, and we waited. It took time for the reply to arrive, and I was afraid that the proposal would be turned down. But Valdas's unfailing tact and diplomacy won the day, and the headmaster graciously consented to the request by the Israeli embassy to hold the award ceremony in the school auditorium in the presence of the children, and to host a small reception after the event.

Of the descendants only three of us – Joy, my son Ze'ev and I – had braved the arctic weather and were in attendance to honor the Levinskas family. But we were swept into the warmth and enthusiasm of the occasion, led by Ambassador Hagit Ben Ya'akov and her entourage from Riga, together with Julius, Valdas and Sarah, members of the Vilnius and Siauliai Jewish communities, and with a very supportive audience of schoolchildren and local Zagareans filling the hall.

The flags of Lithuania and Israel hung on the wall behind the podium. Next to the speakers was a table with a display of photographs of headstones from the Jewish cemeteries of Zagare. This was the project, initiated by Sarah and carried out by the school children, to clean up, decipher and document this last remaining memento of the town's vanished Jewish community.

Leonas and Zofija were already in the hall when we arrived. Joy and I embraced them with much excitement and we all took our seats in the front row. Valdas acted as master of ceremonies, introducing the speakers and translating as needed. Ambassador Ben Ya'akov, visibly moved by the occasion, told her listeners in detail the story of the three righteous gentiles who, seventy years ago, in the darkest days of the Holocaust, had saved Jewish lives. She presented the posthumous award to Leonas, now eighty-four years old. Together with the certificate came the medal, a huge bouquet of flowers, and much applause. Leonas rose to his feet, and with dignity and deep emotion addressed the audience. His words were received with rapt attention. He said that he had learned a lesson from his parents; they had saved people out of humanity, without regard to a person's ethnicity, religion or political views. He told the students that he hoped they would continue to value their country's freedom and ensure that Lithuania would remain a place where everyone could live in safety, regardless of his or her background.

Valdas read out a letter addressed to the Levinskas family from Allan Blacher, the amateur genealogist in London whose family tree of the Trusfus-Yoffe family had enabled me to track down Ruth Yoffe in Jerusalem:

> Although I am not a part of the immediate family of Batya Trusfus, I am writing on their behalf, as a member of the wider Trusfus family, and as someone concerned with documenting and keeping the history of her wider family. It is a great honour for me to have the opportunity to express our heartfelt appreciation to Edvardas and Terese Levinskas and to Terese's sister Lilija, for their extraordinary humanity and their courage. It is impossible in the safety and peace of 2013 to imagine what it must have been like to decide to take the actions they so bravely saw as appropriate in such difficult and dangerous times. The humanity they displayed is almost impossible for us to teach but we must hope that we and our children might learn by pointing to their example and to the real impact it had on saving the lives of members of our actual family. May you and all other descendants they may have enjoy long and healthy lives in the proud memory of such towering examples of human kindness.

For me there was pride and satisfaction in knowing that my encounter with Ruth Yoffe had brought to a conclusion the epic story of her family and that of the Levinskas family. The Righteous among the Nations award presented by Yad Vashem to Leonas Levinskas to honor his parents and aunt was heartwarming testimony that noble and courageous people had lived and acted with true humanity in those terrible times. On our summer day of memorial and dedication, they had been remembered; on this wintry afternoon their heroism was celebrated and formally recognized by Yad Vashem on behalf of the Jewish people.

To a great extent, it seemed as though Zagare had accepted us and we had accepted Zagare. My Israeli-born son, a pilot in the Israel Air Force, the great grandson of Grandpa and Grandma Towb, had joined the fraternity of Litvak descendants – another generation, an added bonus. And somewhere along the road I had unexpectedly acquired a new persona, a new entry to be added to my identity card – that of a Litvak. I remembered my father's fluent Yiddish – he told jokes and stories in a racy Yiddish that was much appreciated by his sisters and his fellow Jews. I now realize that his accent would undoubtedly have been Litvak. And Mother's kitchen specialties were not simply Jewish but rather Litvak cooking. Perhaps it's time for me to start learning Yiddish – the *mammeloshen* – and to add *latkes* and *kugel* and *ptcha* and *tzimmes* to my Friday night family gatherings.

GLOSSARY

aliyah. Immigrating to Israel; lit. ascent (Hebrew).

bar mitzvah. Religious coming of age for a Jewish boy, at age thirteen; lit. son of the commandment (Aramaic and Hebrew).

borscht. Soup traditionally made from beets (Yiddish).

broches. Blessings (Yiddish).

chachmei Zhager. Wise men of Zagare (Yiddish).

challah. Braided Sabbath loaf (Hebrew).

Chanukah. Winter festival of lights (Hebrew).

cheder. Traditional religious primary school; lit. a room (Yiddish).

chuppah. Wedding canopy (Hebrew).

daven. To pray (Yiddish).

der heim. The old country; lit. the home (Yiddish).

gefilte fish. Stuffed fish, usually carp (Yiddish).

goldene medine. America; lit. the golden land (Yiddish).

Haggadah. Order of service for the Passover Seder (Hebrew).

halachah. Jewish religious law; lit. the way (Hebrew).

Ivrit. The Hebrew language (Hebrew).

Kaddish. Prayer said by mourners for the merit of the dead; lit. holy (Aramaic).

kahal. Local Jewish community council in eastern Europe to administer religious, legal and communal affairs (Yiddish).

kashrut. Jewish dietary laws (Hebrew).

kibbutz. Israeli communal farm or settlement (Hebrew).

klezmer. Jewish folk music (Yiddish, from Hebrew *kli*-instrument, *zemer*-song).

kneidlach. Matzah balls for soup (Yiddish).

Kol Nidre. Prayer on eve of Yom Kippur, ushering in Day of Atonement; lit. all vows (Aramaic).

kugel. Baked pudding of potatoes, noodles or similar (Yiddish).

latkes. Fried potato pancakes eaten at Chanukah (Yiddish).

landsman; pl. *landsleit.* Fellow countryman, from the same town or village (Yiddish).

mammeloshen. The Yiddish language; lit. mother tongue (Yiddish).

matzah. Unleavened bread eaten at Pesach (Hebrew).

mazal tov. Congratulations; lit. good luck (Hebrew).

mikve; pl. *mikvaot.* Ritual bath (Hebrew).

minyan. Quorum of ten Jewish males for communal prayer (Hebrew).

mitzvah; pl. *mitzvot.* Religious commandment (Hebrew).

nerot zicharon. Memorial candles (Hebrew).

Pesach. Passover, spring festival commemorating the Exodus from Egypt (Hebrew).

ptcha. Calf's foot jelly (Yiddish).

Seder. Festive combined meal and service for Passover (Hebrew).

Shabbat. Sabbath (Hebrew).

shtetl; pl. *shtetlach.* Small Jewish town or village (Yiddish).

shul. Synagogue (Yiddish).

Talmud. Jewish Oral Law (Hebrew).

Torah. Five Books of Moses, the first books of the Hebrew Bible (Hebrew).

tzimmes. Sweet dish of carrots, dried fruit and meat, cooked slowly (Yiddish).

yahrtzeit. Anniversary of a death; lit. year time (Yiddish).

yichus. Lineage, family pedigree (Yiddish).

Yiddishkeit. Jewishness (Yiddish).

Yom Kippur. Day of Atonement, day of fasting observed in the fall (Hebrew).

FURTHER READING, REFERENCES, SOURCES

BOOKS

Binkiene, Sofija, ed. *Soldiers without Arms*. Vilnius: Mintis, 1967.

Bubnys, Arunas, and D. Kuodyte. *The Holocaust in Lithuania between 1941 and 1944*. Vilnius: Genocide and Resistance Research Center of Lithuania, 2005.

Cassedy, Ellen. *We Are Here: Memories of the Lithuanian Holocaust*. Lincoln: University of Nebraska Press, 2012.

Cohen, Roger. "The Last Jew in Zagare." *New York Times*, November 7, 2011.

Freedman, Rod. *Uncle Chatzkel*, documentary film, 2000, changefocusmedia.com.au.

Goren, Natan et al., eds. *Yahadut Lita* [Lithuanian Jewry]. 4 vols. Tel Aviv: Association of Lithuanian Jews in Israel, 1967–1984.

Greenbaum, Masha. *The Jews of Lithuania: A History of a Remarkable Community, 1316–1945*. Jerusalem: Gefen Publishing House, 1995.

Mazower, Mark. *Dark Continent: Europe's Twentieth Century*. New York: Penguin Books, 1998.

———. *Hitler's Empire: How the Nazis Ruled Europe*. New York: Penguin Books, 2009.

"The Promised Land," in *Big Green Book*, published for the eight hundredth anniversary of the founding of Zagare, 1998.

Richmond, Theo. *Konin: One Man's Quest for a Vanished Jewish Community*. London: Vintage, 1996.

Snyder, Timothy. *Bloodlands: Europe between Hitler and Stalin*. New York: Vintage, 2010.

Wasserstein, Bernard. *On the Eve: The Jews of Europe before the Second World War*. London: Profile Books, 2012.

———. *Vanishing Diaspora: The Jews in Europe since 1945*. London: Penguin Books, 1997.

Yodaiken, Len. *The Judeikins 1998: Family History and Tree*. Kibbutz Kfar Hanasi, 1998.

Zwi, Rose. *Last Walk in Naryshkin Park*. North Melbourne, Victoria: Spinifex Press, 1997.

———. *Once Were Slaves: A Journey through the Circles of Hell*. Darlinghurst, New South Wales: Sydney Jewish Museum, 2010.

WEBSITES AND OTHER RESOURCES

Defending History (edited by Dovid Katz), www.defendinghistory.com

The Jewish Zagare/Zhager Facebook page, https://www.facebook.com/JewishZagare

JewishGen, www.jewishgen.org (see in particular the Zhager ShtetLinks page edited by Cliff Marks, www.kehilalinks.jewishgen.org/zagare)

Yad Vashem Archives, Jerusalem